THE ETHICS OF AMBIGUITY

SIMONE DE BEAUVOIR

The *ETHICS*
OF AMBIGUITY

By

SIMONE DE BEAUVOIR

translated from the French by

BERNARD FRECHTMAN

Citadel Press
Kensington Publishing Corp.
www.kensingtonbooks.com

CITADEL PRESS books are published by

Kensington Publishing Corp.
850 Third Avenue
New York, NY 10022

All Kensington titles, imprints, and distributed lines are available at special quantity discounts for bulk purchases for sales promotions, premiums, fund raising, educational, or institutional use. Special book excerpts or customized printings can also be created to fit specific needs. For details, write or phone the office of the Kensington special sales manager: Kensington Publishing Corp., 850 Third Avenue, New York, NY 10022, attn: Special Sales Department, phone 1-800-221-2647.

First printing 1948

20 19 18 17 16

Printed in the United States of America

ISBN 0-8065-0160-X

Contents

*"Life in itself is neither good nor evil.
It is the place of good and evil,
according to what you make it."*

MONTAIGNE

I. Ambiguity and Freedom

"THE continous work of our life," says Montaigne, "is to build death." He quotes the Latin poets: *Prima, quae vitam dedit, hora corpsit*. And again: *Nascentes morimur*. Man knows and thinks this tragic ambivalence which the animal and the plant merely undergo. A new paradox is thereby introduced into his destiny. "Rational animal," "thinking reed," he escapes from his natural condition without, however, freeing himself from it. He is still a part of this world of which he is a consciousness. He asserts himself as a pure internality against which no external power can take hold, and he also experiences himself as a thing crushed by the dark weight of other things. At every moment he can grasp the non-temporal truth of his existence. But between the past which no longer is and the future which is not yet, this moment when he exists is nothing. This privilege, which he alone possesses, of being a sovereign and unique subject amidst a universe of objects, is what he shares with all his fellow-men. In turn an object for others, he is nothing more than an individual in the collectivity on which he depends.

As long as there have been men and they have lived, they have all felt this tragic ambiguity of their condition, but as long as there have been philosophers and they have thought, most of them have tried to mask it. They have striven to reduce mind to matter, or to reabsorb matter into mind, or to merge them within a single substance.

Those who have accepted the dualism have established a hierarchy between body and soul which permits of considering as negligible the part of the self which cannot be saved. They have denied death, either by integrating it with life or by promising to man immortality. Or, again they have denied life, considering it as a veil of illusion beneath which is hidden the truth of Nirvana.

And the ethics which they have proposed to their disciples has always pursued the same goal. It has been a matter of eliminating the ambiguity by making oneself pure inwardness or pure externality, by escaping from the sensible world or by being engulfed in it, by yielding to eternity or enclosing oneself in the pure moment. Hegel, with more ingenuity, tried to reject none of the aspects of man's condition and to reconcile them all. According to his system, the moment is preserved in the development of time; Nature asserts itself in the face of Spirit which denies it while assuming it; the individual is again found in the collectivity within which he is lost; and each man's death is fulfilled by being canceled out into the Life of Mankind. One can thus repose in a marvelous optimism where even the bloody wars simply express the fertile restlessness of the Spirit.

At the present time there still exist many doctrines which choose to leave in the shadow certain troubling aspects of a too complex situation. But their attempt to lie to us is in vain. Cowardice doesn't pay. Those reasonable metaphysics, those consoling ethics with which they would like to entice us only accentuate the disorder from which we suffer. Men of today seem to feel more acutely than ever the paradox of their condition. They know themselves to be the supreme end to which all action should be subordinated, but the exigencies of action force them to treat one another as instruments or obstacles, as means. The more widespread their mastery of the world, the more they find themselves crushed by uncontrollable forces. Though they are masters of the atomic bomb, yet it is created only to destroy them. Each one has the incomparable taste in his mouth of his own life, and yet each feels himself more insignificant than an insect within the immense collectivity whose limits are one with the earth's. Perhaps in no other age have they manifested their grandeur more brilliantly, and in no other age has this grandeur been so horribly flouted. In spite of so many stubborn lies, at every moment, at every opportunity, the truth comes to light, the truth of life and death, of my solitude and my bond with the world, of my freedom and my servitude, of the insignificance and the sovereign importance of each man and all men. There was Stalingrad and there was Buchenwald, and neither of the two wipes out the other. Since we do not succeed in fleeing it, let us therefore try to look the truth in the face. Let us try to assume our fundamental ambiguity. It is in the knowledge of the genuine conditions of our life that we must draw our strength to live and our reason for acting.

From the very beginning, existentialism defined itself as a philosophy of ambiguity. It was by affirming the irreducible character of ambiguity that Kierkegaard opposed himself to Hegel, and it is by ambiguity that, in our own generation, Sartre, in *Being and Nothingness*, fundamentally defined man, that being whose being is not to be, that subjectivity which realizes itself only as a presence in the world, that engaged freedom, that surging of the for-oneself which is immediately given for others. But it is also claimed that existentialism is a philosophy of the absurd and of despair. It encloses man in a sterile anguish, in an empty subjectivity. It is incapable of furnishing him with any principle for making choices. Let him do as he pleases. In any case, the game is lost. Does not Sartre declare, in effect, that man is a "useless passion," that he tries in vain to realize the synthesis of the for-oneself and the in-oneself, to make himself God? It is true. But it is also true that the most optimistic ethics have all begun by emphasizing the element of failure involved in the condition of man; without failure, no ethics; for a being who, from the very start, would be an exact co-incidence with himself, in a perfect plenitude, the notion of having-to-be would have no meaning. One does not offer an ethics to a God. It is impossible to propose any to man if one defines him as nature, as something given. The so-called psychological or empirical ethics manage to establish themselves only by introducing surreptitiously some flaw within the man-thing which they have first defined. Hegel tells us in the last part of *The Phenomenology of Mind* that moral consciousness can exist only to the extent that there is disagreement between nature and morality. It would disappear if the ethical law became the natural law. To such an extent that by a paradoxical "displacement," if moral

10

action is the absolute goal, the absolute goal is also that moral action may not be present. This means that there can be a having-to-be only for a being who, according to the existentialist definition, questions himself in his being, a being who is at a distance from himself and who has to be his being.

Well and good. But it is still necessary for the failure to be surmounted, and existentialist ontology does not allow this hope. Man's passion is useless; he has no means for becoming the being that he is not. That too is true. And it is also true that in *Being and Nothingness* Sartre has insisted above all on the abortive aspect of the human adventure. It is only in the last pages that he opens up the perspective for an ethics. However, if we reflect upon his descriptions of existence, we perceive that they are far from condemning man without recourse.

The failure described in *Being and Nothingness* is definitive, but it is also ambiguous. Man, Sartre tells us, is "a being who *makes himself* a lack of being *in order that there might be* being." That means, first of all, that his passion is not inflicted upon him from without. He chooses it. It is his very being and, as such, does not imply the idea of unhappiness. If this choice is considered as useless, it is because there exists no absolute value before the passion of man, outside of it, in relation to which one might distinguish the useless from the useful. The word "useful" has not yet received a meaning on the level of description where *Being and Nothingness* is situated. It can be defined only in the human world established by man's projects and the ends he sets up. In the

11

original helplessness from which man surges up, nothing is useful, nothing is useless. It must therefore be understood that the passion to which man has acquiesced finds no external justification. No outside appeal, no objective necessity permits of its being called useful. It *has* no reason to will itself. But this does not mean that it can not justify itself, that it can not *give itself* reasons for being that it does not *have*. And indeed Sartre tells us that man makes himself this lack of being *in order that* there might be being. The term *in order that* clearly indicates an intentionality. It is not in vain that man nullifies being. Thanks to him, being is disclosed and he desires this disclosure. There is an original type of attachment to being which is not the relationship "wanting to be" but rather "wanting to disclose being." Now, here there is not failure, but rather success. This end, which man proposes to himself by making himself lack of being, is, in effect, realized by him. By uprooting himself from the world, man makes himself present to the world and makes the world present to him. I should like to be the landscape which I am contemplating, I should like this sky, this quiet water to think themselves within me, that it might be I whom they express in flesh and bone, and I remain at a distance. But it is also by this distance that the sky and the water exist before me. My contemplation is an excruciation only because it is also a joy. I can not appropriate the snow field where I slide. It remains foreign, forbidden, but I take delight in this very effort toward an impossible possession. I experience it as a triumph, not as a defeat. This means that man, in his vain attempt to *be* God, makes

12

himself exist *as* man, and if he is satisfied with this existence, he coincides exactly with himself. It is not granted him to exist without tending toward this being which he will never be. But it is possible for him to want this tension even with the failure which it involves. His being is lack of being, but this lack has a way of being which is precisely existence. In Hegelian terms it might be said that we have here a negation of the negation by which the positive is re-established. Man makes himself a lack, but he can deny the lack as lack and affirm himself as a positive existence. He then assumes the failure. And the condemned action, insofar as it is an effort to be, finds its validity insofar as it is a manifestation of existence. However, rather than being a Hegelian act of surpassing, it is a matter of a conversion. For in Hegel the surpassed terms are preserved only as abstract moments, whereas we consider that existence still remains a negativity in the positive affirmation of itself. And it does not appear, in its turn, as the term of a further synthesis. The failure is not surpassed, but assumed. Existence asserts itself as an absolute which must seek its justification within itself and not suppress itself, even though it may be lost by preserving itself. To attain his truth, man must not attempt to dispel the ambiguity of his being but, on the contrary, accept the task of realizing it. He rejoins himself only to the extent that he agrees to remain at a distance from himself. This conversion is sharply distinguished from the Stoic conversion in that it does not claim to oppose to the sensible universe a formal freedom which is without content. To exist genuinely is not to

13

deny this spontaneous movement of my transcendence, but only to refuse to lose myself in it. Existentialist conversion should rather be compared to Husserlian reduction: let man put his will to be "in parentheses" and he will thereby be brought to the consciousness of his true condition. And just as phenomenological reduction prevents the errors of dogmatism by suspending all affirmation concerning the mode of reality of the external world, whose flesh and bone presence the reduction does not, however, contest, so existentialist conversion does not suppress my instincts, desires, plans, and passions. It merely prevents any possibility of failure by refusing to set up as absolutes the ends toward which my transcendence thrusts itself, and by considering them in their connection with the freedom which projects them.

The first implication of such an attitude is that the genuine man will not agree to recognize any foreign absolute. When a man projects into an ideal heaven that impossible synthesis of the for-itself and the in-itself that is called God, it is because he wishes the regard of this existing Being to change his existence into being; but if he agrees not to be in order to exist genuinely, he will abandon the dream of an inhuman objectivity. He will understand that it is not a matter of being right in the eyes of a God, but of being right in his own eyes. Renouncing the thought of seeking the guarantee for his existence outside of himself, he will also refuse to believe in unconditioned values which would set themselves up athwart his freedom like things. Value is this lacking-being of which freedom *makes itself* a lack; and it is

14

because the latter makes itself a lack that value appears. It is desire which creates the desirable, and the project which sets up the end. It is human existence which makes values spring up in the world on the basis of which it will be able to judge the enterprise in which it will be engaged. But first it locates itself beyond any pessimism, as beyond any optimism, for the fact of its original springing forth is a pure contingency. Before existence there is no more reason to exist than not to exist. The lack of existence can not be evaluated since it is the fact on the basis of which all evaluation is defined. It can not be compared to anything for there is nothing outside of it to serve as a term of comparison. This rejection of any extrinsic justification also confirms the rejection of an original pessimism which we posited at the beginning. Since it is unjustifiable from without, to declare from without that it is unjustifiable is not to condemn it. And the truth is that outside of existence there is nobody. Man exists. For him it is not a question of wondering whether his presence in the world is useful, whether life is worth the trouble of being lived. These questions make no sense. It is a matter of knowing whether he wants to live and under what conditions.

But if man is free to define for himself the conditions of a life which is valid in his own eyes, can he not choose whatever he likes and act however he likes? Dostoievsky asserted, "If God does not exist, everything is permitted." Today's believers use this formula for their own advantage. To re-establish man at the heart of his destiny is, they claim, to repudiate all ethics. However, far from

Since no God, Man bears responsibility for a world which he makes.

God's absence authorizing all license, the contrary is the case, because man is abandoned on the earth, because his acts are definitive, absolute engagements. He bears the responsibility for a world which is not the work of a strange power, but of himself, where his defeats are inscribed, and his victories as well. A God can pardon, efface, and compensate. But if God does not exist, man's faults are inexpiable. If it is claimed that, whatever the case may be, this earthly stake has no importance, this is precisely because one invokes that inhuman objectivity which we declined at the start. One can not start by saying that our earthly destiny *has* or *has not* importance, for it depends upon us to give it importance. It is up to man to make it important to be a man, and he alone can feel his success or failure. And if it is again said that nothing forces him to try to justify his being in this way, then one is playing upon the notion of freedom in a dishonest way. The believer is also free to sin. The divine law is imposed upon him only from the moment he decides to save his soul. In the Christian religion, though one speaks very little about them today, there are also the damned. Thus, on the earthly plane, a life which does not seek to ground itself will be a pure contingency. But it is permitted to wish to give itself a meaning and a truth, and it then meets rigorous demands within its own heart.

However, even among the proponents of secular ethics, there are many who charge existentialism with offering no objective content to the moral act. It is said that this philosophy is subjective, even solipsistic. If he is once enclosed within himself, how can man get out? But there

16

too we have a great deal of dishonesty. It is rather well known that the fact of being a subject is a universal fact and that the Cartesian *cogito* expresses both the most individual experience and the most objective truth. By affirming that the source of all values resides in the freedom of man, existentialism merely carries on the tradition of Kant, Fichte, and Hegel, who, in the words of Hegel himself, "have taken for their point of departure the principle according to which the essence of right and duty and the essence of the thinking and willing subject are absolutely identical." The idea that defines all humanism is that the world is not a given world, foreign to man, one to which he has to force himself to yield from without. It is the world willed by man, insofar as his will expresses his genuine reality.

Some will answer, "All well and good. But Kant escapes solipsism because for him genuine reality is the human person insofar as it transcends its empirical embodiment and chooses to be universal." And doubtless Hegel asserted that the "right of individuals to their particularity is equally contained in ethical substantiality, since particularity is the extreme, phenomenal modality in which moral reality exists (*Philosophy of Right*, § 154)." But for him particularity appears only as a moment of the totality in which it must surpass itself. Whereas for existentialism, it is not impersonal universal man who is the source of values, but the plurality of concrete, particular men projecting themselves toward their ends on the basis of situations whose particularity is

17

as radical and as irreducible as subjectivity itself. How could men, originally separated, get together?

And, indeed, we are coming to the real situation of the problem. But to state it is not to demonstrate that it can not be resolved. On the contrary, we must here again invoke the notion of Hegelian "displacement." There is an ethics only if there is a problem to solve. And it can be said, by inverting the preceding line of argument, that the ethics which have given solutions by effacing the fact of the separation of men are not valid precisely because there *is* this separation. An ethics of ambiguity will be one which will refuse to deny *a priori* that separate existants can, at the same time, be bound to each other, that their individual freedoms can forge laws valid for all.

Before undertaking the quest for a solution, it is interesting to note that the notion of situation and the recognition of separation which it implies are not peculiar to existentialism. We also meet it in Marxism which, from one point of view, can be considered as an apotheosis of subjectivity. Like all radical humanism, Marxism rejects the idea of an inhuman objectivity and locates itself in the tradition of Kant and Hegel. Unlike the old kind of utopian socialism which confronted earthly order with the archetypes of Justice, Order, and Good, Marx does not consider that certain human situations are, in themselves and absolutely, preferable to others. It is the needs of people, the revolt of a class, which define aims and goals. It is from within a rejected situation, in the light of this rejection, that a new state appears as desirable; only the will of men decides; and it is on the basis of a certain individual act of rooting itself in the historical and economic world that this will thrusts itself toward the future and then chooses a perspective where such words as goal, progress, efficacy, success, failure, action, adversaries, instruments, and obstacles, have a meaning. Then certain acts can be regarded as good and others as bad.

In order for the universe of revolutionary values to arise, a subjective movement must create them in revolt and hope. And this movement appears so essential to Marxists that if an intellectual or a bourgeois also claims to want revolution, they distrust him. They think that it is only from the outside, by abstract recognition, that the bourgeois intellectual can adhere to these values which he himself has not set up. Regardless of what he does, his situation makes it impossible for the ends pursued by proletarians to be absolutely his ends too, since it is not the very impulse of his life which has begotten them.

However, in Marxism, if it is true that the goal and the meaning of action are defined by human wills, these wills do not appear as free. They are the reflection of objective conditions by which the situation of the class or the people under consideration is defined. In the present moment of the development of capitalism, the proletariat can not help wanting its elimination as a class. Subjectivity is re-absorbed into the objectivity of the given world. Revolt, need, hope, rejection, and desire are only the resultants of external forces. The psychology of behavior endeavors to explain this alchemy.

It is known that that is the essential point on which existentialist ontology is opposed to dialectical materialism. We think that the meaning of the situation does not impose itself on the consciousness of a passive subject, that it surges up only by the disclosure which a free subject effects in his project. It appears evident to us that in order to adhere to Marxism, to enroll in a party, and in one rather than another, to be actively attached to it, even a Marxist needs a decision whose source is only in himself. And this autonomy is not the privilege (or the defect) of the intellectual or the bourgeois. The proletariat, taken as a whole, as a class, can become conscious of its situation in more than one way. It can want the revolution to be brought about by one party or another. It can let itself be lured on, as happened to the German proletariat, or can sleep in the dull comfort which capitalism grants it, as does the American proletariat. It may be said that in all these cases it is betraying; still, it must be free to betray. Or, if one pretends to distinguish the real proletariat from a treacherous proletariat, or a misguided or unconscious or mystified one, then it is no longer a flesh and blood proletariat that one is dealing with, but the idea of a proletariat, one of those ideas which Marx ridiculed.

Besides, in practice, Marxism does not *always* deny freedom. The very notion of action would lose all meaning if history were a mechanical unrolling in which man appears only as a passive conductor of outside forces. By

20

acting, as also by preaching action, the Marxist revolutionary asserts himself as a veritable agent; he assumes himself to be free. And it is even curious to note that most Marxists of today — unlike Marx himself — feel no repugnance at the edifying dullness of moralizing speeches. They do not limit themselves to finding fault with their adversaries in the name of historical realism. When they tax them with cowardice, lying, selfishness, and venality, they very well mean to condemn them in the name of a moralism superior to history. Likewise, in the eulogies which they bestow upon each other they exalt the eternal virtues, courage, abnegation, lucidity, integrity. It may be said that all these words are used for propagandistic purposes, that it is only a matter of expedient language. But this is to admit that this language is heard, that it awakens an echo in the hearts of those to whom it is addressed. Now, neither scorn nor esteem would have any meaning if one regarded the acts of a man as a purely mechanical resultant. In order for men to become indignant or to admire, they must be conscious of their own freedom and the freedom of others. Thus, everything occurs within each man and in the collective tactics as if men were free. But then what revelation can a coherent humanism hope to oppose to the testimony which man brings to bear upon himself? So Marxists often find themselves having to confirm this belief in freedom, even if they have to reconcile it with determination as well as they can.

However, while this concession is wrested from them by the very practice of action, it is in the name of action that they attempt to condemn a philosophy of freedom. They declare authoritatively that the existence of freedom would make any concerted enterprise impossible. According to them, if the individual were not constrained by the external world to want this rather than that, there would be nothing to defend him against his whims. Here, in different language, we again meet the charge formulated by the respectful believer of supernatural imperatives. In the eyes of the Marxist, as of the Christian, it seems that to act freely is to give up justifying one's acts. This is a curious reversal of the Kantian "you must; therefore, you can." Kant postulates freedom in the name of morality. The Marxist, on the contrary, declares, "You must; therefore, you can not." To him a man's action seems valid only if the man has not helped set it going by an internal movement. To admit the ontological possibility of a choice is already to betray the Cause. Does this mean that the revolutionary attitude in any way gives up being a moral attitude? It would be logical, since we observed with Hegel that it is only insofar as the choice is not realized at first that it can be set up as a moral choice. But here again Marxist thought hesitates. It sneers at idealistic ethics which do not bite into the world; but its scoffing signifies that there can be no ethics outside of action, not that action lowers itself to the level of a simple natural process. It is quite evident that the revolutionary enterprise has a human meaning. Lenin's remark, which says, in substance, "I call any action useful to the party moral action; I call it immoral if it is harmful to the party," cuts two ways. On the one

22

hand, he refuses to accept outdated values, but he also sees in political operation a total manifestation of man as having-to-be at the same time as being. Lenin refuses to set up ethics abstractly because he means to realize it effectively. And yet a moral idea is present in the words, writings, and acts of Marxists. It is contradictory, then, to reject with horror the moment of choice which is precisely the moment when spirit passes into nature, the moment of the concrete fulfillment of man and morality.

As for us, whatever the case may be, we believe in freedom. Is it true that this belief must lead us to despair? Must we grant this curious paradox: that from the moment a man recognizes himself as free, he is prohibited from wishing for anything?

On the contrary, it appears to us that by turning toward this freedom we are going to discover a principle of action whose range will be universal. The characteristic feature of all ethics is to consider human life as a game that can be won or lost and to teach man the means of winning. Now, we have seen that the original scheme of man is ambiguous: he wants to be, and to the extent that he coincides with this wish, he fails. All the plans in which this will to be is actualized are condemned; and the ends circumscribed by these plans remain mirages. Human transcendence is vainly engulfed in those miscarried attempts. But man also wills himself to be a disclosure of being, and if he coincides with this wish, he wins, for the fact is that the world becomes present by his presence in it. But the disclosure implies a perpetual tension to keep being at a certain distance, to tear oneself from the world, and to assert oneself as a freedom. To wish for the disclosure of the world and to assert oneself as freedom are one and the same movement. Freedom is the source from which all significations and all values spring. It is the original condition of all justification of existence. The man who seeks to justify his life must want freedom itself absolutely and above everything else. At the same time that it requires the realization of concrete ends, of particular projects, it requires itself universally. It is not a ready-made value which offers itself from the outside to my abstract adherence, but it appears (not on the plane of facility, but on the moral plane) as a cause of itself. It is necessarily summoned up by the values which it sets up and through which it sets itself up. It can not establish a denial of itself, for in denying itself, it would deny the possibility of any foundation. To will oneself moral and to will oneself free are one and the same decision.

It seems that the Hegelian notion of "displacement" which we relied on a little while ago is now turning against us. There is ethics only if ethical action is not present. Now, Sartre declares that every man is free, that there is no way of his not being free. When he wants to escape his destiny, he is still freely fleeing it. Does not this presence of a so to speak natural freedom contradict the notion of ethical freedom? What meaning can there be in the words *to will oneself* free, since at the beginning we *are* free? It is contradictory to set freedom up as something conquered if at first it is something given.

This objection would mean something only if freedom

24

were a thing or a quality naturally attached to a thing. Then, in effect, one would either have it or not have it. But the fact is that it merges with the very movement of this ambiguous reality which is called existence and which *is* only by making itself be; to such an extent that it is precisely only by having to be conquered that it gives itself. To will oneself free is to effect the transition from nature to morality by establishing a genuine freedom on the original upsurge of our existence.

Every man is originally free, in the sense that he spontaneously casts himself into the world. But if we consider this spontaneity in its facticity, it appears to us only as a pure contingency, an upsurging as stupid as the clinamen of the Epicurean atom which turned up at any moment whatsoever from any direction whatsoever. And it was quite necessary for the atom to arrive somewhere. But its movement was not justified by this result which had not been chosen. It remained absurd. Thus, human spontaneity always projects itself toward something. The psychoanalyst discovers a meaning even in abortive acts and attacks of hysteria. But in order for this meaning to justify the transcendence which discloses it, it must itself be founded, which it will never be if I do not choose to found it myself. Now, I can evade this choice. We have said that it would be contradictory deliberately to will oneself not free. But one can choose not to will himself free. In laziness, heedlessness, capriciousness, cowardice, impatience, one contests the meaning of the project at the very moment that one defines it. The spontaneity of the subject is then merely a vain living palpitation, its movement toward the object is a flight, and itself is an absence. To convert the absence into presence, to convert my flight into will, I must assume my project positively. It is not a matter of retiring into the completely inner and, moreover, abstract movement of a given spontaneity, but of adhering to the concrete and particular movement by which this spontaneity defines itself by thrusting itself toward an end. It is through this end that it sets up that my spontaneity confirms itself by reflecting upon itself. Then, by a single movement, my will, establishing the content of the act, is legitimized by it. I realize my escape toward the other as a freedom when, assuming the presence of the object, I thereby assume myself before it as a presence. But this justification requires a constant tension. My project is never founded; it founds itself. To avoid the anguish of this permanent choice, one may attempt to flee into the object itself, to engulf one's own presence in it. In the servitude of the serious, the original spontaneity strives to deny itself. It strives in vain, and meanwhile it then fails to fulfill itself as moral freedom.

We have just described only the subjective and formal aspect of this freedom. But we also ought to ask ourselves whether one can will oneself free in any matter, whatsoever it may be. It must first be observed that this will is developed in the course of time. It is in time that the goal is pursued and that freedom confirms itself. And this assumes that it is realized as a unity in the unfolding of time. One escapes the absurdity of the clinamen only by escaping the absurdity of the pure moment. An exist-

26

ence would be unable to found itself if moment by moment it crumbled into nothingness. That is why no moral question presents itself to the child as long as he is still incapable of recognizing himself in the past or seeing himself in the future. It is only when the moments of his life begin to be organized into behaviour that he can decide and choose. The value of the chosen end is confirmed and, reciprocally, the genuineness of the choice is manifested concretely through patience, courage, and fidelity. If I leave behind an act which I have accomplished, it becomes a thing by falling into the past. It is no longer anything but a stupid and opaque fact. In order to prevent this metamorphosis, I must ceaselessly return to it and justify it in the unity of the project in which I am engaged. Setting up the movement of my transcendence requires that I never let it uselessly fall back upon itself, that I prolong it indefinitely. Thus I can not genuinely desire an end today without desiring it through my whole existence, insofar as it is the future of this present moment and insofar as it is the surpassed past of days to come. To will is to engage myself to persevere in my will. This does not mean that I ought not aim at any limited end. I may desire absolutely and forever a revelation of a moment. This means that the value of this provisional end will be confirmed indefinitely. But this living confirmation can not be merely contemplative and verbal. It is carried out in an act. The goal toward which I surpass myself must appear to me as a point of departure toward a new act of surpassing. Thus, a creative freedom develops happily without ever congealing into unjustified

27

facticity. The creator leans upon anterior creations in order to create the possibility of new creations. His present project embraces the past and places confidence in the freedom to come, a confidence which is never disappointed. It discloses being at the end of a further disclosure. At each moment freedom is confirmed through all creation.

 However, man does not create the world. He succeeds in disclosing it only through the resistance which the world opposes to him. The will is defined only by raising obstacles, and by the contingency of facticity certain obstacles let themselves be conquered, and others do not. This is what Descartes expressed when he said that the freedom of man is infinite, but his power is limited. How can the presence of these limits be reconciled with the idea of a freedom confirmimg itself as a unity and an indefinite movement?

In the face of an obstacle which it is impossible to overcome, stubbornness is stupid. If I persist in beating my fist against a stone wall, my freedom exhausts itself in this useless gesture without succeeding in giving itself a content. It debases itself in a vain contingency. Yet, there is hardly a sadder virtue than resignation. It transforms into phantoms and contingent reveries projects which had at the beginning been set up as will and freedom. A young man has hoped for a happy or useful or glorious life. If the man he has become looks upon these miscarried attempts of his adolescence with disillusioned indifference, there they are, forever frozen in the dead past. When an effort fails, one declares bitterly that he has lost time and wasted his powers. The failure condemns that whole part of ourselves which we had engaged in the effort. It was to escape this dilemma that the Stoics preached indifference. We could indeed assert our freedom against all constraint if we agreed to renounce the particularity of our projects. If a door refuses to open, let us accept not opening it and there we are free. But by doing that, one manages only to save an abstract notion of freedom. It is emptied of all content and all truth. The power of man ceases to be limited because it is annulled. It is the particularity of the project which determines the limitation of the power, but it is also what gives the project its content and permits it to be set up. There are people who are filled with such horror at the idea of a defeat that they keep themselves from ever doing anything. But no one would dream of considering this gloomy passivity as the triumph of freedom.

The truth is that in order for my freedom not to risk coming to grief against the obstacle which its very engagement has raised, in order that it might still pursue its movement in the face of the failure, it must, by giving itself a particular content, aim by means of it at an end which is nothing else but precisely the free movement of existence. Popular opinion is quite right in admiring a man who, having been ruined or having suffered an accident, knows how to gain the upper hand, that is, renew his engagement in the world, thereby strongly asserting the independence of freedom in relation to thing. Thus, when the sick Van Gogh calmly accepted the prospect of a future in which he would be unable to paint any more, there was no sterile resignation. For him painting was a personal way of life and of communication with others which in another form could be continued even in an asylum. The past will be integrated and freedom will be confirmed in a renunciation of this kind. It will be lived in both heartbreak and joy. In heartbreak, because the project is then robbed of its particularity — it sacrifices its flesh and blood. But in joy, since at the moment one releases his hold, he again finds his hands free and ready to stretch out toward a new future. But this act of passing beyond is conceivable only if what the content has in view is not to bar up the future, but, on the contrary, to plan new possibilities. This brings us back by another route to what we had already indicated. My freedom must not seek to trap being but to disclose it. The disclosure is the transition from being to existence. The goal which my freedom aims 'at is conquering existence across the always inadequate density of being.

However, such salvation is only possible if, despite obstacles and failures, a man preserves the disposal of his future, if the situation opens up more possibilities to him. In case his transcendence is cut off from his goal or there is no longer any hold on objects which might give it a valid content, his spontaneity is dissipated without founding anything. Then he may not justify his existence positively and he feels its contingency with wretched disgust. There is no more obnoxious way to punish a man than to force him to perform acts which make no sense to him, as when one empties and fills the same ditch indefinitely, when one makes soldiers who are being punished march up and down, or when one forces a schoolboy to copy lines. Revolts broke out in Italy in September 1946 because the unemployed were set to breaking pebbles which served no purpose whatever. As is well known, this was also the weakness which ruined the national workshops in 1848. This mystification of useless effort is more intolerable than fatigue. Life imprisonment is the most horrible of punishments because it preserves existence in its pure facticity but forbids it all legitimation. A freedom can not will itself without willing itself as an indefinite movement. It must absolutely reject the constraints which arrest its drive toward itself. This rejection takes on a positive aspect when the constraint is natural. One rejects the illness by curing it. But it again assumes the negative aspect of revolt when the oppressor is a human freedom. One can not deny being: the in-itself is, and negation has no hold over this being, this pure positivity; one does not escape this fullness: a destroyed house *is* a ruin; a broken chain *is* scrap iron: one attains only signification and, through it, the for-itself which is projected there; the for-itself carries nothingness in its heart and can be annihilated, whether in the very upsurge of its existence or through the world in which it exists. The prison is repudiated as such when the prisoner escapes. But revolt, insofar as it is pure negative movement, remains abstract. It is fulfilled as freedom only by returning to the positive, that is, by giving itself a content through action, escape, political struggle, revolution. Human transcendence then seeks, with the destruction of the given situation, the whole future which will flow from its victory. It resumes its

31

indefinite rapport with itself. There are limited situations where this return to the positive is impossible, where the future is radically blocked off. Revolt can then be achieved only in the definitive rejection of the imposed situation, in suicide.

It can be seen that, on the one hand, freedom can always save itself, for it is realized as a disclosure of existence through its very failures, and it can again confirm itself by a death freely chosen. But, on the other hand, the situations which it discloses through its project toward itself do not appear as equivalents. It regards as privileged situations those which permit it to realize itself as indefinite movement; that is, it wishes to pass beyond everything which limits its power; and yet, this power is always limited. Thus, just as life is identified with the will-to-live, freedom always appears as a movement of liberation. It is only by prolonging itself through the freedom of others that it manages to surpass death itself and to realize itself as an indefinite unity. Later on we shall see what problems such a relationship raises. For the time being it is enough for us to have established the fact that the words "to will oneself free" have a positive and concrete meaning. If man wishes to save his existence, as only he himself can do, his original spontaneity must be raised to the height of moral freedom by taking itself as an end through the disclosure of a particular content.

But a new question is immediately raised. If man has one and only one way to save his existence, how can he choose not to choose it in all cases? How is a bad willing possible? We meet with this problem in all ethics, since it is precisely the possibility of a perverted willing which gives a meaning to the idea of virtue. We know the answer of Socrates, of Plato, of Spinoza: "No one is willfully bad." And if Good is a transcendent thing which is more or less foreign to man, one imagines that the mistake can be explained by error. But if one grants that the moral world is the world genuinely willed by man, all possibility of error is eliminated. Moreover, in Kantian ethics, which is at the origin of all ethics of autonomy, it is very difficult to account for an evil will. As the choice of his character which the subject makes is achieved in the intelligible world by a purely rational will, one can not understand how the latter expressly rejects the law which it gives to itself. But this is because Kantism defined man as a pure positivity, and it therefore recognized no other possibility in him than coincidence with himself. We, too, define morality by this adhesion to the self; and this is why we say that man can not positively decide between the negation and the assumption of his freedom, for as soon as he decides, he assumes it. He can not positively will not to be free for such a willing would be self-destructive. Only, unlike Kant, we do not see man as being essentially a positive will. On the contrary, he is first defined as a negativity. He is first at a distance from himself. He can coincide with himself only by agreeing never to rejoin himself. There is within him a perpetual playing with the negative, and he thereby escapes himself, he escapes his freedom. And it is precisely because an evil will is here possible that the words "to will oneself free" have a meaning. Therefore, not only do we assert that the existentialist doctrine permits the elaboration of an ethics, but it even appears to us as the only philosophy in which an ethics has its place. For, in a metaphysics of transcendence, in the classical sense of the term, evil is reduced to error; and in humanistic philosophies it is impossible to account for it, man being defined as complete in a complete world. Existentialism alone gives — like religions — a real role to evil, and it is this, perhaps, which make its judgments so gloomy. Men do not like to feel themselves in danger. Yet, it is because there are real dangers, real failures and real earthly damnation that words like victory, wisdom, or joy have meaning. Nothing is decided in advance, and it is because man has something to lose and because he can lose that he can also win.

Therefore, in the very condition of man there enters the possibility of not fulfilling this condition. In order to fulfill it he must assume himself as a being who "makes himself a lack of being so that there might be being." But the trick of dishonesty permits stopping at any moment whatsoever. One may hesitate to make oneself a lack of being, one may withdraw before existence, or one may falsely assert oneself as being, or assert oneself as nothingness. One may realize his freedom only as an abstract independence, or, on the contrary, reject with despair the distance which separates us from being. All errors are possible since man is a negativity, and they are motivated by the anguish he feels in the face of his freedom. Concretely, men slide incoherently from one attitude to another. We shall limit ourselves to describing in their abstract form those which we have just indicated.

Man's unhappiness, says Descartes, is due to his having
first been a child. And indeed the unfortunate choices
which most men make can only be explained by the fact
that they have taken place on the basis of childhood. The
child's situation is characterized by his finding himself
cast into a universe which he has not helped to establish,
which has been fashioned without him, and which appears to him as an absolute to which he can only submit.
In his eyes, human inventions, words, customs, and values
are given facts, as inevitable as the sky and the trees. This
means that the world in which he lives is a serious world,
since the characteristic of the spirit of seriousness is to
consider values as ready-made things. That does not mean
that the child himself is serious. On the contrary, he is
allowed to play, to expend his existence freely. In his
child's circle he feels that he can passionately pursue and
joyfully attain goals which he has set up for himself. But
if he fulfills this experience in all tranquillity, it is precisely because the domain open to his subjectivity seems
insignificant and puerile in his own eyes. He feels himself
happily irresponsible. The real world is that of adults
where he is allowed only to respect and obey. The naive
victim of the mirage of the for-others, he believes in the
being of his parents and teachers. He takes them for the

divinities which they vainly try to be and whose appearance they like to borrow before his ingenuous eyes. Rewards, punishments, prizes, words of praise or blame instill in him the conviction that there exist a good and an evil which like a sun and a moon exist as ends in themselves. In his universe of definite and substantial things, beneath the sovereign eyes of grown-up persons, he thinks that he too has *being* in a definite and substantial way. He is a good little boy or a scamp; he enjoys being it. If something deep inside him belies his conviction, he conceals this imperfection. He consoles himself for an inconsistency which he attributes to his young age by pinning his hopes on the future. Later on he too will become a big imposing statue. While waiting, he plays at being, at being a saint, a hero, a guttersnipe. He feels himself like those models whose images are sketched out in his books in broad, unequivocal strokes: explorer, brigand, sister of charity. This game of being serious can take on such an importance in the child's life that he himself actually becomes serious. We know such children who are caricatures of adults. Even when the joy of existing is strongest, when the child abandons himself to it, he feels himself protected against the risk of existence by the ceiling which human generations have built over his head. And it is by virtue of this that the child's condition (although it can be unhappy in other respects) is metaphysically privileged. Normally the child escapes the anguish of freedom. He can, if he likes, be recalcitrant, lazy; his whims and his faults concern only him. They do not weigh upon the earth. They can not make a dent in the serene order of a world which existed before him, without him, where he is in a state of security by virtue of his very insignificance. He can do with impunity whatever he likes. He knows that nothing can ever happen through him; everything is already given; his acts engage nothing, not even himself.

There are beings whose life slips by in an infantile world because, having been kept in a state of servitude and ignorance, they have no means of breaking the ceiling which is stretched over their heads. Like the child, they can exercise their freedom, but only within this universe which has been set up before them, without them. This is the case, for example, of slaves who have not raised themselves to the consciousness of their slavery. The southern planters were not altogether in the wrong in considering the negroes who docilely submitted to their paternalism as "grown-up children." To the extent that they respected the world of the whites the situation of the black slaves was exactly an infantile situation. This is also the situation of women in many civilizations; they can only submit to the laws, the gods, the customs, and the truths created by the males. Even today in western countries, among women who have not had in their work an apprenticeship of freedom, there are still many who take shelter in the shadow of men; they adopt without discussion the opinions and values recognized by their husband or their lover, and that allows them to develop childish qualities which are forbidden to adults because they are based on a feeling of irresponsibility. If what is called women's futility often has so much charm and grace, if it sometimes has a genuinely moving character, it is because it manifests a pure and gratuitous taste for existence, like the games of children; it is the absence of the serious. The unfortunate thing is that in many cases this thoughtlessness, this gaiety, these charming inventions imply a deep complicity with the world of men which they seem so graciously to be contesting, and it is a mistake to be astonished, once the structure which shelters them seems to be in danger, to see sensitive, ingenuous, and light-minded women show themselves harder, more bitter, and even more furious or cruel than their masters. It is then that we discover the difference which distinguishes them from an actual child: the child's situation is imposed upon him, whereas the woman (I mean the western woman of today) chooses it or at least consents to it. Ignorance and error are facts as inescapable as prison walls. The negro slave of the eighteenth century, the Mohammedan woman enclosed in a harem have no instrument, be it in thought or by astonishment or anger, which permits them to attack the civilization which oppresses them. Their behavior is defined and can be judged only within this given situation, and it is possible that in this situation, limited like every human situation, they realize a perfect assertion of their freedom. But once there appears a possibility of liberation, it is resignation of freedom not to exploit the possibility, a resignation which implies dishonesty and which is a positive fault.

The fact is that it is very rare for the infantile world to maintain itself beyond adolescence. From childhood on, flaws begin to be revealed in it. With astonishment, revolt and disrespect the child little by little asks himself, "Why must I act that way? What good is it? And what will happen if I act in another way?" He discovers his subjectivity; he discovers that of others. And when he arrives at the age of adolescence he begins to vacillate because he notices the contradictions among adults as well as their hesitations and weakness. Men stop appearing as if they were gods, and at the same time the adolescent discovers the human character of the reality about him. Language, customs, ethics, and values have their source in these uncertain creatures. The moment has come when he too is going to be called upon to participate in their operation; his acts weigh upon the earth as much as those of other men. He will have to choose and decide. It is comprehensible that it is hard for him to live this moment of his history, and this is doubtless the deepest reason for the crisis of adolescence; the individual must at last assume his subjectivity.

From one point of view the collapsing of the serious world is a deliverance. Although he was irresponsible, the child also felt himself defenseless before obscure powers which directed the course of things. But whatever the joy of this liberation may be, it is not without great confusion that the adolescent finds himself cast into a world which is no longer ready-made, which has to be made; he is abandoned, unjustified, the prey of a freedom that is no longer chained up by anything. What will he do in the face of this new situation? This is the moment when he decides. If what might be called the natural history of an individual, his affective complexes, etcetera

39

depend above all upon his childhood, it is adolescence which appears as the moment of moral choice. Freedom is then revealed and he must decide upon his attitude in the face of it. Doubtless, this decision can always be reconsidered, but the fact is that conversions are difficult because the world reflects back upon us a choice which is confirmed through this world which it has fashioned. Thus, a more and more rigorous circle is formed from which one is more and more unlikely to escape. Therefore, the misfortune which comes to man as a result of the fact that he was a child is that his freedom was first concealed from him and that all his life he will be nostalgic for the time when he did not know its exigencies.

This misfortune has still another aspect. Moral choice is free, and therefore unforeseeable. The child does not contain the man he will become. Yet, it is always on the basis of what he has been that a man decides upon what he wants to be. He draws the motivations of his moral attitude from within the character which he has given himself and from within the universe which is its correlative. Now, the child set up this character and this universe little by little, without foreseeing its development. He was ignorant of the disturbing aspect of this freedom which he was heedlessly exercising. He tranquilly abandoned himself to whims, laughter, tears, and anger which seemed to him to have no morrow and no danger, and yet which left ineffaceable imprints about him. The drama of original choice is that it goes on moment by moment for an entire lifetime, that it occurs without reason, before any reason, that freedom is there as if it were

40

present only in the form of contingency. This contingency recalls, in a way, the arbitrariness of the grace distributed by God in Calvinistic doctrine. Here too there is a sort of predestination issuing not from an external tyranny but from the operation of the subject itself. Only, we think that man has always a possible recourse to himself. There is no choice so unfortunate that he cannot be saved.

It is in this moment of justification — a moment which extends throughout his whole adult life — that the attitude of man is placed on a moral plane. The contingent spontaneity can not be judged in the name of freedom. Yet a child already arouses sympathy or antipathy. Every man casts himself into the world by making himself a lack of being; he thereby contributes to reinvesting it with human signification. He discloses it. And in this movement even the most outcast sometimes feel the joy of existing. They then manifest existence as a happiness and the world as a source of joy. But it is up to each one to make himself a lack of more or less various, profound, and rich aspects of being. What is called vitality, sensitivity, and intelligence are not ready-made qualities, but a way of casting oneself into the world and of disclosing being. Doubtless, every one casts himself into it on the basis of his physiological possibilities, but the body itself is not a brute fact. It expresses our relationship to the world, and that is why it is an object of sympathy or repulsion. And on the other hand, it *determines* no behavior. There is vitality only by means of free generosity. Intelligence supposes good will, and, inversely, a man is never stupid if he adapts his language and his behavior to his capacities, and sensitivity is nothing else but the presence which is attentive to the world and to itself. The reward for these spontaneous qualities issues from the fact that they make significances and goals appear in the world. They discover reasons for existing. They confirm us in the pride and joy of our destiny as man. To the extent that they subsist in an individual they still arouse sympathy, even if he has made himself hateful by the meaning which he has given to his life. I have heard it said that at the Nuremberg trial Goering exerted a certain seductive power on his judges because of the vitality which emanated from him.

If we were to try to establish a kind of hierarchy among men, we would put those who are denuded of this living warmth — the tepidity which the Gospel speaks of — on the lowest rung of the ladder. To exist is to *make oneself* a lack of being; it is to *cast* oneself into the world. Those who occupy themselves in restraining this original movement can be considered as sub-men. They have eyes and ears, but from their childhood on they make themselves blind and deaf, without love and without desire. This apathy manifests a fundamental fear in the face of existence, in the face of the risks and tensions which it implies. The sub-man rejects this "passion" which is his human condition, the laceration and the failure of that drive toward being which always misses its goal, but which thereby is the very existence which he rejects.

Such a choice immediately confirms itself. Just as a bad painter, by a single movement, paints bad paintings and is satisfied with them, whereas in a work of value the

42

artist immediately recognizes the demand of a higher sort of work, in like fashion the original poverty of his project exempts the sub-man from seeking to legitimize it. He discovers around him only an insignificant and dull world. How could this naked world arouse within him any desire to feel, to understand, to live? The less he exists, the less is there reason for him to exist, since these reasons are created only by existing.

Yet, he exists. By the fact of transcending himself he indicates certain goals, he circumscribes certain values. But he at once effaces these uncertain shadows. His whole behavior tends toward an elimination of their ends. By the incoherence of his plans, by his haphazard whims, or by his indifference, he reduces to nothingness the meaning of his surpassing. His acts are never positive choices, only flights. He can not prevent himself from being a presence in the world, but he maintains this presence on the plane of bare facticity.

However, if a man were permitted to be a brute fact, he would merge with the trees and pebbles which are not aware that they exist; we would consider these opaque lives with indifference. But the sub-man arouses contempt, that is, one recognizes him to be responsible for himself at the moment that one accuses him of not willing himself. The fact is that no man is a datum which is passively suffered; the rejection of existence is still another way of existing; nobody can know the peace of the tomb while he is alive. There we have the defeat of the sub-man. He would like to forget himself, to be ignorant of himself, but the nothingness which is at the heart of

43

man is also the consciousness that he has of himself. His negativity is revealed positively as anguish, desire, appeal, laceration, but as for the genuine return to the positive, the sub-man eludes it. He is afraid of engaging himself in a project as he is afraid of being disengaged and thereby of being in a state of danger before the future, in the midst of its possibilities. He is thereby led to take refuge in the ready-made values of the serious world. He will proclaim certain opinions; he will take shelter behind a label; and to hide his indifference he will readily abandon himself to verbal outbursts or even physical violence. One day, a monarchist, the next day, an anarchist, he is more readily anti-semitic, anti-clerical, or anti-republican. Thus, though we have defined him as a denial and a flight, the sub-man is not a harmless creature. He realizes himself in the world as a blind uncontrolled force which anybody can get control of. In lynchings, in pogroms, in all the great bloody movements organized by the fanaticism of seriousness and passion, movements where there is no risk, those who do the actual dirty work are recruited from among the sub-men. That is why every man who wills himself free within a human world fashioned by free men will be so disgusted by the sub-men. Ethics is the triumph of freedom over facticity, and the sub-man feels only the facticity of his existence. Instead of aggrandizing the reign of the human, he opposes his inert resistance to the projects of other men. No project has meaning in the world disclosed by such an existence. Man is defined as a wild flight. The world about him is bare and incoherent. Nothing ever happens; nothing

44

merits desire or effort. The sub-man makes his way across a world deprived of meaning toward a death which merely confirms his long negation of himself. The only thing revealed in this experience is the absurd facticity of an existence which remains forever unjustified if it has not known how to justify itself.

The sub-man experiences the desert of the world in his boredom. And the strange character of a universe with which he has created no bond also arouses fear in him. Weighted down by present events, he is bewildered before the darkness of the future which is haunted by frightful specters, war, sickness, revolution, fascism, bolshevism. The more indistinct these dangers are, the more fearful they become. The sub-man is not very clear about what he has to lose, since he has nothing, but this very uncertainty re-enforces his terror. Indeed, what he fears is that the shock of the unforeseen may remind him of the agonizing consciousness of himself.

Thus, fundamental as a man's fear in the face of existence may be, though he has chosen from his earliest years to deny his presence in the world, he can not keep himself from existing, he can not efface the agonizing evidence of his freedom. That is why, as we have just seen, in order to get rid of his freedom, he is led to engage it positively. The attitude of the sub-man passes logically over into that of the serious man; he forces himself to submerge his freedom in the content which the latter accepts from society. He loses himself in the object in order to annihilate his subjectivity. This certitude has been described so frequently that it will not be necessary to consider it at length. Hegel has spoken of it ironically. In *The Phenomenology of Mind* he has shown that the sub-man plays the part of the inessential in the face of the object which is considered as the essential. He suppresses himself to the advantage of the Thing, which, sanctified by respect, appears in the form of a Cause, science, philosophy, revolution, etc. But the truth is that this ruse miscarries, for the Cause can not save the individual insofar as he is a concrete and separate existence. After Hegel, Kierkegaard and Nietzsche also railed at the deceitful stupidity of the serious man and his universe. And *Being and Nothingness* is in large part a description of the serious man and his universe. The serious man gets rid of his freedom by claiming to subordinate it to values which would be unconditioned. He imagines that the accession to these values likewise permanently confers value upon himself. Shielded with "rights," he fulfills himself as a *being* who is escaping from the stress of existence. The serious is not defined by the nature of the ends pursued. A frivolous lady of fashion can have this mentality of the serious as well as an engineer. There is the serious from the moment that freedom denies itself to the advantage of ends which one claims are absolute.

Since all of this is well known, I should like to make only a few remarks in this place. It is easily understood why, of all the attitudes which are not genuine, the latter is the most widespread; because every man was first a child. After having lived under the eyes of the gods, having been given the promise of divinity, one does not

46

readily accept becoming simply a man with all his anxiety and doubt. What is to be done? What is to be believed? Often the young man, who has not, like the sub-man, first rejected existence, so that these questions are not even raised, is nevertheless frightened at having to answer them. After a more or less long crisis, either he turns back toward the world of his parents and teachers or he adheres to the values which are new but seem to him just as sure. Instead of assuming an affectivity which would throw him dangerously beyond himself, he represses it. Liquidation, in its classic form of transference and sublimation, is the passage from the affective to the serious in the propitious shadow of dishonesty. The thing that matters to the serious man is not so much the nature of the object which he prefers to himself, but rather the fact of being able to lose himself in it. So much so, that the movement toward the object is, in fact, through his arbitrary act the most radical assertion of subjectivity: to believe for belief's sake, to will for will's sake is, detaching transcendence from its end, to realize one's freedom in its empty and absurd form of freedom of indifference.

The serious man's dishonesty issues from his being obliged ceaselessly to renew the denial of this freedom. He chooses to live in an infantile world, but to the child the values are really given. The serious man must mask the movement by which he gives them to himself, like the mythomaniac who while reading a love-letter pretends to forget that she has sent it to herself. We have already pointed out that certain adults can live in the

Circumstances can make the world appear as given → e.g. economic, social, being a woman

universe of the serious in all honesty, for example, those who are denied all instruments of escape, those who are enslaved or who are mystified. The less economic and social circumstances allow an individual to act upon the world, the more this world appears to him as given. This is the case of women who inherit a long tradition of submission and of those who are called "the humble." There is often laziness and timidity in their resignation; their honesty is not quite complete; but to the extent that it exists, their freedom remains available, it is not denied. They can, in their situation of ignorant and powerless individuals, know the truth of existence and raise themselves to a properly moral life. It even happens that they turn the freedom which they have thus won against the very object of their respect; thus, in *A Doll's House*, the childlike naivete of the heroine leads her to rebel against the lie of the serious. On the contrary, the man who has the necessary instruments to escape this lie and who does not want to use them consumes his freedom in denying them. He makes himself serious. He dissimulates his subjectivity under the shield of rights which emanate from the ethical universe recognized by him; he is no longer a man, but a father, a boss, a member of the Christian Church or the Communist Party.

If one denies the subjective tension of freedom one is evidently forbidding himself universally to will freedom in an indefinite movement. By virtue of the fact that he refuses to recognize that he is freely establishing the value of the end he sets up, the serious man makes himself the slave of that end. He forgets that every goal is

Serious man makes the slave of an end

48

at the same time a point of departure and that human freedom is the ultimate, the unique end to which man should destine himself. He accords an absolute meaning to the epithet *useful*, which, in truth, has no more meaning if taken by itself than the words *high, low, right*, and *left*. It simply designates a relationship and requires a complement: useful *for* this or that. The complement itself must be put into question, and, as we shall see later on, the whole problem of action is then raised.

But the serious man puts nothing into question. For the military man, the army is useful; for the colonial administrator, the highway; for the serious revolutionary, the revolution — army, highway, revolution, productions becoming inhuman idols to which one will not hesitate to sacrifice man himself. Therefore, the serious man is dangerous. It is natural that he makes himself a tyrant. Dishonestly ignoring the subjectivity of his choice, he pretends that the unconditioned value of the object is being asserted through him; and by the same token he also ignores the value of the subjectivity and the freedom of others, to such an extent that, sacrificing them to the thing, he persuades himself that what he sacrifices is nothing. The colonial administrator who has raised the highway to the stature of an idol will have no scruple about assuring its construction at the price of a great number of lives of the natives; for, what value has the life of a native who is incompetent, lazy, and clumsy when it comes to building highways? The serious leads to a fanaticism which is as formidable as the fanaticism of passion. It is the fanaticism of the Inquisition which

fanaticism

does not hesitate to impose a credo, that is, an internal movement, by means of external constraints. It is the fanaticism of the Vigilantes of America who defend morality by means of lynchings. It is the political fanaticism which empties politics of all human content and imposes the State, not *for* individuals, but *against* them.

In order to justify the contradictory, absurd, and outrageous aspects of this kind of behavior, the serious man readily takes refuge in disputing the serious, but it is the serious of others which he disputes, not his own. Thus, the colonial administrator is not unaware of the trick of irony. He contests the importance of the happiness, the comfort, the very life of the native, but he reveres the Highway, the Economy, the French Empire; he reveres himself as a servant of these divinities. Almost all serious men cultivate an expedient levity; we are familiar with the genuine gaiety of Catholics, the fascist "sense of humor." There are also some who do not even feel the need for such a weapon. They hide from themselves the incoherence of their choice by taking flight. As soon as the Idol is no longer concerned, the serious man slips into the attitude of the sub-man. He keeps himself from existing because he is not capable of existing without a guarantee. Proust observed with astonishment that a great doctor or a great professor often shows himself, outside of his specialty, to be lacking in sensitivity, intelligence, and humanity. The reason for this is that having abdicated his freedom, he has nothing else left but his techniques. In domains where his techniques are not applicable, he either adheres to the most ordinary of values or fulfills himself as a flight. The serious man stubbornly engulfs his transcendence in the object which bars the horizon and bolts the sky. The rest of the world is a faceless desert. Here again one sees how such a choice is immediately confirmed. If there *is* being only, for example, in the form of the Army, how could the military man wish for anything else than to multiply barracks and maneuvers? No appeal rises from the abandoned zones where nothing can be reaped because nothing has been sown. As soon as he leaves the staff, the old general becomes dull. That is why the serious man's life loses all meaning if he finds himself cut off from his ends. Ordinarily, he does not put all his eggs into one basket, but if it happens that a failure or old age ruins all his justifications, then, unless there is a conversion, which is always possible, he no longer has any relief except in flight; ruined, dishonored, this important personage is now only a "has-been." He joins the sub-man, unless by suicide he once and for all puts an end to the agony of his freedom.

It is in a state of fear that the serious man feels this dependence upon the object; and the first of virtues, in his eyes, is prudence. He escapes the anguish of freedom only to fall into a state of preoccupation, of worry. Everything is a threat to him, since the thing which he has set up as an idol is an externality and is thus in relationship with the whole universe and consequently threatened by the whole universe; and since, despite all precautions, he will never be the master of this exterior world to which he has consented to submit, he will be constantly upset by the uncontrollable course of events.

51

He will always be saying that he is disappointed, for his wish to have the world harden into a thing is belied by the very movement of life. The future will contest his present successes; his children will disobey him, his will will be opposed by those of strangers; he will be a prey to ill-humor and bitterness. His very successes have a taste of ashes, for the serious is one of those ways of trying to realize the impossible synthesis of the in-itself and the for-itself. The serious man wills himself to be a god; but he is not one and knows it. He wishes to rid himself of his subjectivity, but it constantly risks being unmasked; it is unmasked. Transcending all goals, reflection wonders, "What's the use?" There then blazes forth the absurdity of a life which has sought outside of itself the justifications which it alone could give itself. Detached from the freedom which might have genuinely grounded them, all the ends that have been pursued appear arbitrary and useless.

This failure of the serious sometimes brings about a radical disorder. Conscious of being unable to be anything, man then decides to be nothing. We shall call this attitude nihilistic. The nihilist is close to the spirit of seriousness, for instead of realizing his negativity as a living movement, he conceives his annihilation in a substantial way. He wants to *be* nothing, and this nothing that he dreams of is still another sort of being, the exact Hegelian antithesis of being, a stationary datum. Nihilism is disappointed seriousness which has turned back upon itself. A choice of this kind is not encountered among those who, feeling the joy of existence, assume its gratuity. It appears either at the moment of adolescence, when the individual, seeing his child's universe flow away, feels the lack which is in his heart, or, later on, when the attempts to fulfill himself as a being have failed; in any case, among men who wish to rid themselves of the anxiety of their freedom by denying the world and themselves. By this rejection, they draw near to the sub-man. The difference is that their withdrawal is not their original movement. At first, they cast themselves into the world, sometimes even with a largeness of spirit. They exist and they know it.

It sometimes happens that, in his state of deception, a man maintains a sort of affection for the serious world; this is how Sartre describes Baudelaire in his study of the poet. Baudelaire felt a burning rancor in regard to the values of his childhood, but this rancor still involved some respect. Scorn alone liberated him. It was necessary for him that the universe which he rejected continue in order for him to detest it and scoff at it; it is the attitude of the demoniacal man as Jouhandeau has also described him: one stubbornly maintains the values of childhood, of a society, or of a Church in order to be able to trample upon them. The demoniacal man is still very close to the serious; he wants to believe in it; he confirms it by his very revolt; he feels himself as a negation and a freedom, but he does not realize this freedom as a positive liberation.

One can go much further in rejection by occupying himself not in scorning but in annihilating the rejected world and himself along with it. For example, the man who gives himself to a cause which he knows to be lost chooses to merge the world with one of its aspects which carries within it the germ of its ruin, involving himself in this condemned universe and condemning himself with it. Another man devotes his time and energy to an undertaking which was not doomed to failure at the start but which he himself is bent on ruining. Still another rejects each of his projects one after the other, frittering them away in a series of caprices and thereby systematically annuling the ends which he is aiming at. The constant negation of the word by the word, of the act by the act, of art by art was realized by Dadaist incoherence. By following a strict injunction to commit disorder and anarchy, one achieved the abolition of all behavior, and therefore of all ends and of oneself.

But this will to negation is forever belying itself, for it manifests itself as a presence at the very moment that it displays itself. It therefore implies a constant tension, inversely symmetrical with the existential and more painful tension, for if it is true that man is not, it is also true that he exists, and in order to realize his negativity positively he will have to contradict constantly the movement of existence. If one does not resign himself to suicide one slips easily into a more stable attitude than the shrill rejection of nihilism. Surrealism provides us with a historical and concrete example of different possible kinds of evolution. Certain initiates, such as Vache and Crevel, had recourse to the radical solution of suicide. Others destroyed their bodies and ruined their minds by drugs. Other succeeded in a sort of moral suicide; by dint of depopulating the world around them, they found themselves in a desert, with themselves reduced to the level of the sub-man; they no longer try to flee, they are fleeing. There are also some who have again sought out the security of the serious. They have reformed, arbitrarily choosing marriage, politics, or religion as refuges. Even the surrealists who have wanted to remain faithful to themselves have been unable to avoid returning to the positive, to the serious. The negation of aesthetic, spiritual, and moral values has become an ethics; unruliness has become a rule. We have been present at the establishment of a new Church, with its dogmas, its rites, its faithful, its priests, and even its martyrs; today, there is nothing of the destroyer in Breton; he is a pope. And as every assassination of painting is still a painting, a lot of surrealists have found themselves the authors of positive works; their revolt has become the matter on which their career has been built. Finally, some of them, in a genuine return to the positive, have been able to realize their freedom; they have given it a content without disavowing it. They have engaged themselves, without losing themselves, in political action, in intellectual or artistic research, in family or social life.

The attitude of the nihilist can perpetuate itself as such only if it reveals itself as a positivity at its very core. Rejecting his own existence, the nihilist must also reject the existences which confirm it. If he wills himself to be nothing, all mankind must also be annihilated; otherwise, by means of the presence of this world that the Other reveals he meets himself as a presence in the world. But this thirst for destruction immediately takes the form of a desire for power. The taste of nothingness joins the original taste of being whereby every man is first defined; he realizes himself as a being by making himself that by which nothingness comes into the world. Thus, Nazism was both a will for power and a will for suicide at the same time. From a historical point of view, Nazism has many other features besides; in particular, beside the dark romanticism which led Rauschning to entitle his work *The Revolution of Nihilism*, we also find a gloomy seriousness. The fact is that Nazism was in the service of petit bourgeois seriousness. But it is interesting to note that its ideology did not make this alliance impossible, for the serious often rallies to a partial nihilism, denying everything which is not its object in order to hide from itself the antinomies of action.

A rather pure example of this impassioned nihilism is the well-known case of Drieu la Rochelle. *The Empty Suitcase* is the testimony of a young man who acutely felt the fact of existing as a lack of being, of not being. This is a genuine experience on the basis of which the only possible salvation is to assume the lack, to side with the man who exists against the idea of a God who does not. On the contrary — a novel like *Gilles* is proof — Drieu stubbornly persisted in his deception. In his hatred of himself he chose to reject his condition as a man, and this led him to hate all men along with himself. Gilles knows satisfaction only when he fires on Spanish workers and sees the flow of blood which he compares to the redeeming blood of Christ; as if the only salvation by man were the death of other men, whereby perfect negation is achieved. It is natural that this path ended in collaboration, the ruin of a detested world being merged for Drieu with the annulment of himself. An external failure led him to give to his life a conclusion which it called for dialectically: suicide.

The nihilist attitude manifests a certain truth. In this attitude one experiences the ambiguity of the human condition. But the mistake is that it defines man not as the positive existence of a lack, but as a lack at the heart of existence, whereas the truth is that existence is not a lack as such. And if freedom is experienced in this case in the form of rejection, it is not genuinely fulfilled. The nihilist is right in thinking that the world *possesses* no justification and that he himself *is* nothing. But he forgets that it is up to him to justify the world and to make himself exist validly. Instead of integrating death into life, he sees in it the only truth of the life which appears to him as a disguised death. However, there is life, and the nihilist knows that he is alive. That's where his failure lies. He rejects existence without managing to eliminate it. He denies any meaning to his transcendence, and yet he transcends himself. A man who delights in freedom can find an ally in the nihilist because they contest the serious world together, but he also sees in him an enemy insofar as the nihilist is a systematic rejection of the world and man, and if this rejection ends up in a positive desire for destruction, it then establishes a tyranny which freedom must stand up against.

The fundamental fault of the nihilist is that, challenging all given values, he does not find, beyond their ruin, the importance of that universal, absolute end which freedom itself is. It is possible that, even in this failure, a man may nevertheless keep his taste for an existence which he originally felt as a joy. Hoping for no justification, he will nevertheless take delight in living. He will not turn aside from things which he does not believe in. He will seek a pretext in them for a gratuitous display of activity. Such a man is what is generally called an adventurer. He throws himself into his undertakings with zest, into exploration, conquest, war, speculation, love, politics, but he does not attach himself to the end at which he aims; only to his conquest. He likes action for its own sake. He finds joy in spreading through the world a freedom which remains indifferent to its content. Whether the taste for adventure appears to be based on nihilistic despair or whether it is born directly from the experience of the happy days of childhood, it always implies that freedom is realized as an independence in regard to the serious world and that, on the other hand, the ambiguity of existence is felt not as a lack but in its positive aspect. This attitude dialectically envelops nihilism's opposition to the serious and the opposition to nihilism by existence as such. But, of course, the concrete history of an individual does not necessarily espouse this dialectic, by virtue of the fact that his condition is wholly present to him at each moment and because his freedom before it is, at every moment, total. From the time of his adolescence a man can define himself as an adventurer. The union of an original, abundant vitality and a reflective scepticism will particularly lead to this choice.

It is obvious that this choice is very close to a genuinely moral attitude. The adventurer does not propose to be; he deliberately makes himself a lack of being; he aims expressly at existence; though engaged in his undertaking, he is at the same time detached from the goal. Whether he succeeds or fails, he goes right ahead throwing himself into a new enterprise to which he will give himself with the same indifferent ardor. It is not from things that he expects the justification of his choices. Considering such behavior at the moment of its subjectivity, we see that it conforms to the requirements of ethics, and if existentialism were solipsistic, as is generally claimed, it would have to regard the adventurer as its perfect hero.

First of all, it should be noticed that the adventurer's attitude is not always pure. Behind the appearance of caprice, there are many men who pursue a secret goal in utter seriousness; for example, fortune or glory. They proclaim their scepticism in regard to recognized values. They do not take politics seriously. They thereby allow themselves to be collaborationists in '41 and communists in '45, and it is true they don't give a hang about the interests of the French people or the proletariat; they are attached to their career, to their success. This *arrivisme* is at the very antipodes of the spirit of adventure; because the zest for existence is then never experienced in its gratuity. It also happens that the genuine love for adventure is inextricably mixed with an attachment to the values of the serious. Cortez and the conquistadores served God and the emperor by serving their own pleasure. Ad-

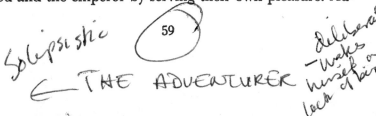

Solipsistic

← THE ADVENTURER

deliberately
- makes
himself or
lack of being.

venture can also be shot through with passion. The taste for conquest is often subtly tied up with the taste for possession. Was seduction all that Don Juan liked? Did he not also like women? Or was he not even looking for a woman capable of satisfying him?

But even if we consider adventure in its purity, it appears to us to be satisfying only at a subjective moment, which, in fact, is a quite abstract moment. The adventurer always meets others along the way; the conquistador meets the Indians; the condottiere hacks out a path through blood and ruins; the explorer has comrades about him or soldiers under his orders; every Don Juan is confronted with Elviras. Every undertaking unfolds in a human world and affects men. What distinguishes adventure from a simple game is that the adventurer does not limit himself to asserting his existence in solitary fashion. He asserts it in relationship to other existences. He has to declare himself.

Two attitudes are possible. He can become conscious of the real requirements of his own freedom, which can will itself only by destining itself to an open future, by seeking to extend itself by means of the freedom of others. Therefore, in any case, the freedom of other men must be respected and they must be helped to free themselves. Such a law imposes limits upon action and at the same time immediately gives it a content. Beyond the rejected seriousness is found a genuine seriousness. But the man who acts in this way, whose end is the liberation of himself and others, who forces himself to respect this end through the means which he uses to attain it, no longer deserves the name of adventurer. One would not dream for example, of applying it to a Lawrence, who was so concerned about the lives of his companions and the freedom of others, so tormented by the human problems which all action raises. One is then in the presence of a genuinely free man.

The man we call an adventurer, on the contrary, is one who remains indifferent to the content, that is, to the human meaning of his action, who thinks he can assert his own existence without taking into account that of others. The fate of Italy mattered very little to the Italian condottiere; the massacres of the Indians meant nothing to Pizarro; Don Juan was unaffected by Elvira's tears. Indifferent to the ends they set up for themselves, they were still more indifferent to the means of attaining them; they cared only for their pleasure or their glory. This implies that the adventurer shares the nihilist's contempt for men. And it is by this very contempt that he believes he breaks away from the contemptible condition in which those who do not imitate his pride are stagnating. Thus, nothing prevents him from sacrificing these insignificant beings to his own will for power. He will treat them like instruments; he will destroy them if they get in his way. But meanwhile he appears as an enemy in the eyes of others. His undertaking is not only an individual wager; it is a combat. He can not win the game without making himself a tyrant or a hangman. And as he can not impose this tyranny without help, he is obliged to serve the regime which will allow him to exercise it. He needs money, arms, soldiers, or the support of the police and the laws. It is not a matter of chance, but a dialectical necessity which leads the adventurer to be complacent regarding all regimes which defend the privilege of a class or a party, and more particularly authoritarian regimes and fascism. He needs fortune, leisure, and enjoyment, and he will take these goods as supreme ends in order to be prepared to remain free in regard to any end. Thus, confusing a quite external availability with real freedom, he falls, with a pretext of independence, into the servitude of the object. He will range himself on the side of the regimes which guarantee him his privileges, and he will prefer those which confirm him in his contempt regarding the common herd. He will make himself its accomplice, its servant, or even its valet, alienating a freedom which, in reality, can not confirm itself as such if it does not wear its own face. In order to have wanted to limit it to itself, in order to have emptied it of all concrete content, he realizes it only as an abstract independence which turns into servitude. He must submit to masters unless he makes himself the supreme master. Favorable circumstances are enough to transform the adventurer into a dictator. He carries the seed of one within him, since he regards mankind as indifferent matter destined to support the game of his existence. But what he then knows is the supreme servitude of tyranny.

Hegel's criticism of the tyrant is applicable to the adventurer to the extent that he is himself a tyrant, or at the very least an accomplice of the oppressor. No man can save himself alone. Doubtless, in the very heat of an action the adventurer can know a joy which is sufficient unto itself, but once the undertaking is over and has congealed behind him into a thing, it must, in order to remain alive, be animated anew by a human intention which must transcend it toward the future into recognition or admiration. When he dies, the adventurer will be surrendering his whole life into the hands of men; the only meaning it will have will be the one they confer upon it. He knows this since he talks about himself, often in books. For want of a work, many desire to bequeath their own personality to posterity: at least during their lifetime they need the approval of a few faithful. Forgotten and detested, the adventurer loses the taste for his own existence. Perhaps without his knowing it, it seems so precious to him because of others. It willed itself to be an affirmation, an example to all mankind. Once it falls back upon itself, it becomes futile and unjustified.

Thus, the adventurer devises a sort of moral behavior because he assumes his subjectivity positively. But if he dishonestly refuses to recognize that this subjectivity necessarily transcends itself toward others, he will enclose himself in a false independence which will indeed be servitude. To the free man he will be only a chance ally in whom one can have no confidence; he will easily become an enemy. His fault is believing that one can do something for oneself without others and even against them.

The passionate man is, in a way, the antithesis of the adventurer. In him too there is a sketch of the synthesis of freedom and its content. But in the adventurer it is the content which does not succeed in being genuinely fulfilled. Whereas in the passionate man it is subjectivity which fails to fulfill itself genuinely.

What characterizes the passionate man is that he sets up the object as an absolute, not, like the serious man, as a thing detached from himself, but as a thing disclosed by his subjectivity. There are transitions between the serious and passion. A goal which was first willed in the name of the serious can become an object of passion; inversely, a passionate attachment can wither into a serious relationship. But real passion asserts the subjectivity of its involvement. In amorous passion particularly, one does not want the beloved being to be admired objectively; one prefers to think her unknown, unrecognized; the lover thinks that his appropriation of her is greater if he is alone in revealing her worth. That is the genuine thing offered by all passion. The moment of subjectivity therein vividly asserts itself, in its positive form, in a movement toward the object. It is only when passion has been degraded to an organic need that it ceases to choose itself. But as long as it remains alive it does so because subjectivity is animating it; if not pride, at least complacency and obstinacy. At the same time that it is an assumption of this subjectivity, it is also a disclosure of being. It helps populate the world with desirable objects, with exciting meanings. However, in the passions which we shall call maniacal, to distinguish them from the generous passions, freedom does not find its genuine form. The passionate man seeks possession; he seeks to attain being. The failure and the hell which he creates for himself have been described often enough. He causes certain rare treasures to appear in the world, but he also depopulates it. Nothing exists outside of his stubborn project; therefore nothing can induce him to modify his choices. And having involved his whole life with an external object which can continually escape him, he tragically feels his dependence. Even if it does not definitely disappear, the object never gives itself. The passionate man makes himself a lack of being not that there might *be* being, but in order to be. And he remains at a distance; he is never fulfilled.

That is why though the passionate man inspires a certain admiration, he also inspires a kind of horror at the same time. One admires the pride of a subjectivity which chooses its end without bending itself to any foreign law and the precious brilliance of the object revealed by the force of this assertion. But one also considers the solitude in which this subjectivity encloses itself as injurious. Having withdrawn into an unusual region of the world, seeking not to communicate with other men, this freedom is realized only as a separation. Any conversation, any relationship with the passionate man is impossible. In the eyes of those who desire a communion of freedom, he therefore appears as a stranger, an obstacle. He opposes an opaque resistance to the movement of freedom which wills itself infinite. The passionate man is not only an inert facticity. He too is on the way to tyranny. He knows that his will emanates only from him, but he can nevertheless attempt to impose it upon others. He authorizes himself to do that by a partial nihilism. Only the object of his passion appears real and full to him. All the rest are insignificant. Why not betray, kill, grow violent? It is never *nothing* that one destroys. The whole universe is perceived only as an ensemble of means or obstacles through which it is a matter of attaining the thing in which one has engaged his being. Not intending his freedom for men, the passionate man does not recognize them as freedoms either. He will not hesitate to treat them as things. If the object of his passion concerns the world in general, this tyranny becomes fanaticism. In all fanatical movements there exists an element of the serious. The values invented by certain men in a passion of hatred, fear, or faith are thought and willed by others as given realities. But there is no serious fanaticism which does not have a passional base, since all adhesion to the serious world is brought about by repressed tendencies and complexes. Thus, maniacal passion represents a damnation for the one who chooses it, and for other men it is one of the forms of separation which disunites freedoms. It leads to struggle and oppression. A man who seeks being far from other men, seeks it against them at the same time that he loses himself.

Yet, a conversion can start within passion itself. The cause of the passionate man's torment is his distance from the object; but he must accept it instead of trying to eliminate it. It is the condition within which the object is disclosed. The individual will then find his joy in the very wrench which separates him from the being of which he makes himself a lack. Thus, in the letters of Mademoiselle de Lespinasse there is constant passing from grief to the assumption of this grief. The lover describes her tears and her tortures, but she asserts that she loves this unhappiness. It is also a source of delight for her. She likes the other to appear as another through her separation. It pleases her to exalt, by her very suffering, that strange existence which she chooses to set up as worthy of any sacrifice. It is only as something strange, forbidden, as something free, that the other is revealed as an other. And to love him genuinely is to love him in his otherness and in that freedom by which he escapes. Love is then renunciation of all possession, of all confusion. One renounces being in order that there may be that being which one is not. Such generosity, moreover, can not be exercised on behalf of any object whatsoever. One can not love a pure thing in its independence and its separation, for the thing does not have positive independence. If a man prefers the land he has discovered to the possession of this land, a painting or a statue to their material presence, it is insofar as they appear to him as possibilities open to other men. Passion is converted to genuine freedom only if one destines his existence to other existences through the being — whether thing or man — at which he aims, without hoping to entrap it in the destiny of the in-itself.

Thus, we see that no existence can be validly fulfilled if it is limited to itself. It appeals to the existence of others. The idea of such a dependence is frightening, and the separation and multiplicity of existants raises highly disturbing problems. One can understand that men who are aware of the risks and the inevitable element of failure involved in any engagement in the world attempt to fulfill themselves outside of the world. Man is permitted to separate himself from this world by contemplation, to think about it, to create it anew. Some men, instead of building their existence upon the indefinite unfolding of time, propose to assert it in its eternal aspect and to achieve it as an absolute. They hope, thereby, to surmount the ambiguity of their condition. Thus, many intellectuals seek their salvation either in critical thought or creative activity.

We have seen that the serious contradicts itself by the fact that not everything can be taken seriously. It slips into a partial nihilism. But nihilism is unstable. It tends to return to the positive. Critical thought attempts to militate everywhere against all aspects of the serious but without foundering in the anguish of pure negation. It sets up a superior, universal, and timeless value, objective truth. And, correlatively, the critic defines himself positively as the independence of the mind. Crystallizing the negative movement of the criticism of values into a positive reality, he also crystallizes the negativity proper to all mind into a positive presence. Thus, he thinks that he himself escapes all earthly criticism. He does not have to choose between the highway and the native, between America and Russia, between production and freedom. He understands, dominates, and rejects, in the name of total truth, the necessarily partial truths which every human engagement discloses. But ambiguity is at the heart of his very attitude, for the independent man is still a man with his particular situation in the world, and what he defines as objective truth is the object of his own choice. His criticisms fall into the world of particular men. He does not merely describe. He takes sides. If he does not assume the subjectivity of his judgment, he is inevitably caught in the trap of the serious. Instead of the independent mind he claims to be, he is only the shameful servant of a cause to which he has not chosen to rally.

The artist and the writer force themselves to surmount existence in another way. They attempt to realize it as an absolute. What makes their effort genuine is that they do not propose to attain being. They distinguish themselves thereby from an engineer or a maniac. It is existence which they are trying to pin down and make eternal. The word, the stroke, the very marble indicate the object insofar as it is an absence. Only, in the work of art the lack of being returns to the positive. Time is stopped, clear forms and finished meanings rise up. In this return, existence is confirmed and establishes its own justification. This is what Kant said when he defined art as "a finality without end." By virtue of the fact that he has thus set up an absolute object, the creator is then tempted to consider himself as absolute. He justifies the world and therefore thinks he has no need of anyone to justify himself. If the work becomes an idol whereby the artist thinks that he is fulfilling himself as being, he is closing himself up in the universe of the serious; he is falling into the illusion which Hegel exposed when he described the race of "intellectual animals."

There is no way for a man to escape from this world. It is in this world that — avoiding the pitfalls we have just pointed out — he must realize himself morally. Freedom must project itself toward its own reality through a content whose value it establishes. An end is valid only by a return to the freedom which established it and which willed itself through this end. But this will implies that freedom is not to be engulfed in any goal; neither is it to dissipate itself vainly without aiming at a goal. It is not necessary for the subject to seek to be, but it must desire that there *be* being. To will oneself free and to will that there be *being* are one and the same choice, the choice that man makes of himself as a presence in the world. We can neither say that the free man wants freedom in order to desire being, nor that he wants the disclosure of being by freedom. These are two aspects of a single reality. And whichever be the one under consideration, they both imply the bond of each man with all others.

This bond does not immediately reveal itself to everybody. A young man wills himself free. He wills that there be being. This spontaneous liberality which casts him ardently into the world can ally itself to what is commonly called egoism. Often the young man perceives only that aspect of his relationship to others whereby others appear as enemies. In the preface to *The Inner Experience* Georges Bataille emphasizes very forcefully that each individual wants to be All. He sees in every other man and particularly in those whose existence is asserted with most brilliance, a limit, a condemnation of himself. "Each consciousness," said Hegel, "seeks the death of the other." And indeed at every moment others are stealing the whole world away from me. The first movement is to hate them.

But this hatred is naive, and the desire immediately struggles against itself. If I were really everything there would be nothing beside me; the world would be empty. There would be nothing to possess, and I myself would be nothing. If he is reasonable, the young man immediately understands that by taking the world away from me, others also give it to me, since a thing is given to me only by the movement which snatches it from me. To will that there be being is also to will that there be men by and for whom the world is endowed with human significations. One can reveal the world only on a basis revealed by other men. No project can be defined except by its interference with other projects. To make being "be" is to communicate with others by means of being.

This truth is found in another form when we say that freedom can not will itself without aiming at an open future. The ends which it gives itself must be unable to be transcended by any reflection, but only the freedom of other men can extend them beyond our life. I have tried to show in *Pyrrhus and Cineas* that every man needs the freedom of other men and, in a sense, always wants it, even though he may be a tyrant; the only thing he fails to do is to assume honestly the consequences of such a wish. Only the freedom of others keeps each one of us from hardening in the absurdity of facticity. And if we are to believe the Christian myth of creation, God himself was in agreement on this point with the existentialist doctrine since, in the words of an anti-fascist priest, "He had such respect for man that He created him free."

Thus, it can be seen to what an extent those people

are mistaken — or are lying — who try to make of existentialism a solipsism, like Nietzsche, would exalt the bare will to power. According to this interpretation, as widespread as it is erroneous, the individual, knowing himself and choosing himself as the creator of his own values, would seek to impose them on others. The result would be a conflict of opposed wills enclosed in their solitude. But we have seen that, on the contrary, to the extent that passion, pride, and the spirit of adventure lead to this tyranny and its conflicts, existentialist ethics condems them; and it does so not in the name of an abstract law, but because, if it is true that every project emanates from subjectivity, it is also true that this subjective movement establishes by itself a surpassing of subjectivity. Man can find a justification of his own existence only in the existence of other men. Now, he needs such a justification; there is no escaping it. Moral anxiety does not come to man from without; he finds within himself the anxious question, "What's the use?" Or, to put it better, he himself is this urgent interrogation. He flees it only by fleeing himself, and as soon as he exists he answers. It may perhaps be said that it is for *himself* that he is moral, and that such an attitude is egotistical. But there is no ethics against which this charge, which immediately destroys itself, can not be leveled; for how can I worry about what does not concern me? I concern others and they concern me. There we have an irreducible truth. The me-others relationship is as indissoluble as the subject-object relationship.

At the same time the other charge which is often di-

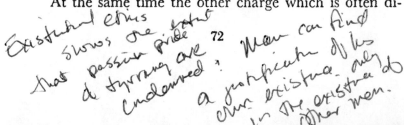

Existential ethics shows that passion pride & tyranny are condemned. Man can find a justification of his own existence only in the existence of other men.

72

rected at existentialism also collapses: of being a formal doctrine, incapable of proposing any content to the freedom which it wants engaged. To will oneself free is also to will others free. This will is not an abstract formula. It points out to each person concrete action to be achieved. But the others are separate, even opposed, and the man of good will sees concrete and difficult problems arising in his relations with them. It is this positive aspect of morality that we are now going to examine.

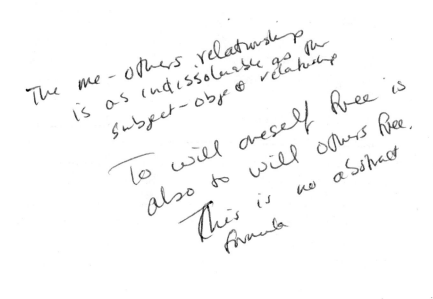

The me - others relationship is as indissoluble as the subject-object relationship

To will oneself free is also to will others free. This is no abstract formula

III. The Positive Aspect of Ambiguity

1. The Aesthetic Attitude

Thus, every man has to do with other men. The world in which he engages himself is a human world in which each object is penetrated with human meanings. It is a speaking world from which solicitations and appeals rise up. This means that, through this world, each individual can give his freedom a concrete content. He must disclose the world with the purpose of further disclosure and by the same movement try to free men, by means of whom the world takes on meaning. But we shall find here the same objection that we met when we examined the abstract moment of individual ethics. If every man *is* free, he can not *will* himself free. Likewise the objection will be raised that he can will nothing for another since that other is free in all circumstances; men are always disclosing being, in Buchenwald as well as in the blue isles of the Pacific, in hovels as well as in palaces; something is always happening in the world, and in the movement of keeping being at a distance, can one not consider its different transformations with a detached joy, or find reasons for acting? No solution is better or worse than any other.

We may call this attitude aesthetic because the one who adopts it claims to have no other relation with the

world than that of detached contemplation; outside of
time and far from men, he faces history, which he thinks
he does not belong to, like a pure beholding; this impersonal version equalizes all situations; it apprehends them
only in the indifference of their differences; it excludes
any preference.

Thus, the lover of historical works is present at the
birth and the downfall of Athens, Rome, and Byzantium
with the same serene passion. The tourist considers the
arena of the Coliseum, the Latifundia of Syracuse, the
thermal baths, the palaces, the temples, the prisons, and
the churches with the same tranquil curiosity: these things
existed, that is enough to satisfy him. Why not also consider with impartial interest those that exist today? One
finds this temptation among many Italians who are
weighed down by a magical and deceptive past; the present already seems to them like a future past. Wars, civil
disputes, invasions and slavery have succeeded one another in their land. Each moment of that tormented history is contradicted by the following one; and yet in the
very midst of this vain agitation there arose domes, sta-
tues, bas-reliefs, paintings and palaces which have remained intact through the centuries and which still en-
chant the men of today. One can imagine an intellectual
Florentine being skeptical about the great uncertain movements which are stirring up his country and which will
die out as did the seethings of the centuries which have
gone by: as he sees it, the important thing is merely to
understand the temporary events and through them to
cultivate that beauty which perishes not. Many French-

men also sought relief in this thought in 1940 and the years which followed. "Let's try to take the point of view of history," they said upon learning that the Germans had entered Paris. And during the whole occupation certain intellectuals sought to keep "aloof from the fray" and to consider impartially contingent facts which did not concern them.

But we note at once that such an attitude appears in moments of discouragement and confusion; in fact, it is a position of withdrawal, a way of fleeing the truth of the present. As concerns the past, this eclecticism is legitimate; we are no longer in a live situation in regard to Athens, Sparta, or Alexandria, and the very idea of a choice has no meaning. But the present is not a potential past; it is the moment of choice and action; we can not avoid living it through a project; and there is no project which is purely contemplative since one always projects himself toward something, toward the future; to put oneself "outside" is still a way of living the inescapable fact that one is inside; those French intellectuals who, in the name of history, poetry, or art, sought to rise above the drama of the age, were willy-nilly its actors; more or less explicitly, they were playing the occupier's game. Likewise, the Italian aesthete, occupied in caressing the marbles and bronzes of Florence, is playing a political role in the life of his country by his very inertia. One can not justify all that is by asserting that everything may equally be the object of contemplation, since man never contemplates: he does.

It is for the artist and the writer that the problem

is raised in a particularly acute and at the same time equivocal manner, for then one seeks to set up the indifference of human situations not in the name of pure contemplation, but of a definite project: the creator projects toward the work of art a subject which he justifies insofar as it is the matter of this work; any subject may thus be admitted, a massacre as well as a masquerade. This aesthetic justification is sometimes so striking that it betrays the author's aim; let us say that a writer wants to communicate the horror inspired in him by children working in sweatshops; he produces so beautiful a book that, enchanted by the tale, the style, and the images, we forget the horror of the sweatshops or even start admiring it. Will we not then be inclined to think that if death, misery, and injustice can be transfigured for our delight, it is not an evil for there to be death, misery, and injustice?

But here too we must not confuse the present with the past. With regard to the past, no further action is possible. There have been war, plague, scandal, and treason, and there is no way of our preventing their having taken place; the executioner became an executioner and the victim underwent his fate as a victim without us; all that we can do is to reveal it, to integrate it into the human heritage, to raise it to the dignity of the aesthetic existence which bears within itself its finality; but first this history had to occur: it occurred as scandal, revolt, crime, or sacrifice, and we were able to try to save it only because it first offered us a form. Today must also exist before being confirmed in its

77

existence: it exists only as an engagement and a commitment. If we first considered the world as an object to be manifested, if we thought that it was saved by this destination in such a way that everything about it already seemed justified and that there was no more of it to reject, then there would also be nothing to say about it, for no form would take shape in it; it is revealed only through rejection, desire, hate and love. In order for the artist to have a world to express he must first be situated in this world, oppressed or oppressing, resigned or rebellious, a man among men. But at the heart of his existence he finds the exigence which is common to all men; he must first will freedom within himself and universally; he must try to conquer it: in the light of this project situations are graded and reasons for acting are made manifest.

2. Freedom and Liberation

One of the chief objections leveled against existentialism is that the precept "to will freedom" is only a hollow formula and offers no concrete content for action. But that is because one has begun by emptying the word freedom of its concrete meaning; we have already seen that freedom realizes itself only by engaging itself in the world: to such an extent that man's project toward freedom is embodied for him in definite acts of behavior.

To will freedom and to will to disclose being are one and the same choice; hence, freedom takes a positive

78

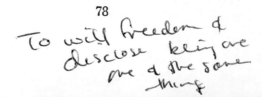
To will freedom & disclose being are one & the same thing

and constructive step which causes being to pass to existence in a movement which is constantly surpassed. Science, technics, art, and philosophy are indefinite conquests of existence over being; it is by assuming themselves as such that they take on their genuine aspect; it is in the light of this assumption that the word progress finds its veridical meaning. It is not a matter of approaching a fixed limit: absolute Knowledge or the happiness of man or the perfection of beauty; all human effort would then be doomed to failure, for with each step forward the horizon recedes a step; for man it is a matter of pursuing the expansion of his existence and of retrieving this very effort as an absolute.

Science condemns itself to failure when, yielding to the infatuation of the serious, it aspires to attain being, to contain it, and to possess it; but it finds its truth if it considers itself as a free engagement of thought in the given, aiming, at each discovery, not at fusion with the thing, but at the possibility of new discoveries; what the mind then projects is the concrete accomplishment of its freedom. The attempt is sometimes made to find an objective justification of science in technics; but ordinarily the mathematician is concerned with mathematics and the physicist with physics, and not with their applications. And, furthermore, technics itself is not objectively justified; if it sets up as absolute goals the saving of time and work which it enables us to realize and the comfort and luxury which it enables us to have access to, then it appears useless and absurd, for the time that one gains can not be accumulated in a storehouse; it is contradictory to want to save up existence, which, the fact is, exists only by being spent, and there is a good case for showing that airplanes, machines, the telephone, and the radio do not make men of today happier than those of former times. But actually it is not a question of giving men time and happiness, it is not a question of stopping the movement of life: it is a question of fulfilling it. If technics is attempting to make up for this lack, which is at the very heart of existence, it fails radically; but it escapes all criticism if one admits that, through it, existence, far from wishing to repose in the security of being, thrusts itself ahead of itself in order to thrust itself still farther ahead, that it aims at an indefinite disclosure of being by the transformation of the thing into an instrument and at the opening of ever new possibilities for man. As for art, we have already said that it should not attempt to set up idols; it should reveal existence as a reason for existing; that is really why Plato, who wanted to wrest man away from the earth and assign him to the heaven of Ideas, condemned the poets; that is why every humanism on the other hand, crowns them with laurels. Art reveals the transitory as an absolute; and as the transitory existence is perpetuated through the centuries, art too, through the centuries, must perpetuate this never-to-be-finished revelation. Thus, the constructive activities of man take on a valid meaning only when they are assumed as a movement toward freedom; and reciprocally, one sees that such a movement is concrete: discoveries, inventions, industries, culture, paintings, and books people the world

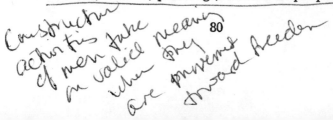

Construction
activities
of men take
on valid meaning
when they
are movement
toward freedom

concretely and open concrete possibilities to men.

Perhaps it is permissible to dream of a future when men will know no other use of their freedom than this free unfurling of itself; constructive activity would be possible for all; each one would be able to aim positively through his projects at his own future. But today the fact is that there are men who can justify their life only by a negative action. As we have already seen, every man transcends himself. But it happens that this transcendence is condemned to fall uselessly back upon itself because it is cut off from its goals. That is what defines a situation of oppression. Such a situation is never natural: man is never oppressed by things; in any case, unless he is a naive child who hits stones or a mad prince who orders the sea to be thrashed, he does not rebel against things, but only against other men. The resistance of the thing sustains the action of man as air sustains the flight of the dove; and by projecting himself through it man accepts its being an obstacle; he assumes the risk of a setback in which he does not see a denial of his freedom. The explorer knows that he may be forced to withdraw before arriving at his goal; the scientist, that a certain phenomenon may remain obscure to him; the technician, that his attempt may prove abortive: these withdrawals and errors are another way of disclosing the world. Certainly, a material obstacle may cruelly stand in the way of an undertaking: floods, earthquakes, grasshoppers, epidemics and plague are scourges; but here we have one of the truths of Stoicism: a man must assume even these misfortunes, and since he must never resign himself in favor of any *thing*, no destruction of a thing will ever be a radical ruin for him; even his death is not an evil since he is man only insofar as he is mortal: he must assume it as the natural limit of his life, as the risk implied by every step. Only man can be an enemy for man; only he can rob him of the meaning of his acts and his life because it also belongs only to him alone to confirm it in its existence, to recognize it in actual fact as a freedom. It is here that the Stoic distinction between "things which do not depend upon us" and those which "depend upon us" proves to be insufficient: for "we" is legion and not an individual; each one depends upon others, and what happens to me by means of others depends upon me as regards its meaning; one does not submit to a war or an occupation as he does to an earthquake: he must take sides for or against, and the foreign wills thereby become allied or hostile. It is this interdependence which explains why oppression is possible and why it is hateful. As we have seen, my freedom, in order to fulfill itself, requires that it emerge into an open future: it is other men who open the future to me, it is they who, setting up the world of tomorrow, define my future; but if, instead of allowing me to participate in this constructive movement, they oblige me to consume my transcendence in vain, if they keep me below the level which they have conquered and on the basis of which new conquests will be achieved, then they are cutting me off from the future, they are changing me into a thing. Life is occupied in both perpetuating itself and in surpassing itself; if all it does

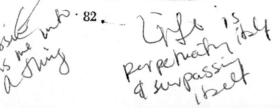

is maintain itself, then living is only not dying, and human existence is indistinguishable from an absurd vegetation; a life justifies itself only if its effort to perpetuate itself is integrated into its surpassing and if this surpassing has no other limits than those which the subject assigns himself. Oppression divides the world into two clans: those who enlighten mankind by thrusting it ahead of itself and those who are condemned to mark time hopelessly in order merely to support the collectivity; their life is a pure repetition of mechanical gestures; their leisure is just about sufficient for them to regain their strength; the oppressor feeds himself on their transcendence and refuses to extend it by a free recognition. The oppressed has only one solution: to deny the harmony of that mankind from which an attempt is made to exclude him, to prove that he is a man and that he is free by revolting against the tyrants. In order to prevent this revolt, one of the ruses of oppression is to camouflage itself behind a natural situation since, after all, one can not revolt against nature. When a conservative wishes to show that the proletariat is not oppressed, he declares that the present distribution of wealth is a natural fact and that there is thus no means of rejecting it; and doubtless he has a good case for proving that, strictly speaking, he is not *stealing* from the worker the product of his labor, since the word *theft* supposes social conventions which in other respects authorizes this type of exploitation; but what the revolutionary means by this word is that the present regime is a human fact. As such, it has to be rejected. This rejection cuts off the will of the oppressor, in his turn, from the future toward which he was hoping to thrust himself alone: another future is substituted, that of revolution. The struggle is not one of words and ideologies; it is real and concrete: if it is this future which triumphs, and not the former, then it is the oppressed who is realized as a positive and open freedom and the oppressor who becomes an obstacle and a thing.

There are thus two ways of surpassing the given: it is something quite different from taking a trip or escaping from prison. In these two cases the given is present in its surpassing; but in one case it is present insofar as it is accepted, in the other insofar as rejected, and that makes a radical difference. Hegel has confused these two movements with the ambiguous term "aufheben"; and the whole structure of an optimism which denies failure and death rests on this ambiguity; that is what allows one to regard the future of the world as a continuous and harmonious development; this confusion is the source and also the consequence; it is a perfect epitome of that idealistic and verbose flabbiness with which Marx charged Hegel and to which he opposed a realistic toughness. Revolt is not integrated into the harmonious development of the world; it does not wish to be integrated but rather to explode at the heart of the world and to break its continuity. It is no accident if Marx defined the attitude of the proletariat not positively but negatively: he does not show it as affirming itself or as seeking to realize a classless society, but rather as first attempting to put an end to itself as a class. And it is precisely because it has no other issue than a negative one that this situation must be eliminated.

All men are interested in this elimination, the oppressor as well as the oppressed, as Marx himself has said, for each one needs to have all men free. There are cases where the slave does not know his servitude and where it is necessary to bring the seed of his liberation to him from the outside: his submission is not enough to justify the tyranny which is imposed upon him. The slave is submissive when one has succeeded in mystifying him in such a way that his situation does not seem to him to be imposed by men, but to be immediately given by nature, by the gods, by the powers against whom revolt has no meaning; thus, he does not accept his condition through a resignation of his freedom since he can not even dream of any other; and in his relationships with his friends, for example, he can live as a free and moral man within this world where his ignorance has enclosed him. The conservative will argue from this that this peace should not be disturbed; it is not necessary to give education to the people or comfort to the natives of the colonies; the "ringleaders" should be suppressed; that is the meaning of an old story of Maurras: there is no need to awaken the sleeper, for that would be to awaken him to unhappiness. Certainly it is not a question of throwing men in spite of themselves, under the pretext of liberation, into a new world, one which they have not chosen, on which they have no grip. The proponents of slavery in the Carolinas had a good case when they showed the conquerors old negro slaves who were be-

85

wildered by a freedom which they didn't know what to
do with and who cried for their former masters; these
false liberations — though in a certain sense they are
inevitable — overwhelm those who are their victims as
if they were a new blow of blind fate. What must be
done is to furnish the ignorant slave with the means of
transcending his situation by means of revolt, to put an
end to his ignorance. We know that the problem of the
nineteenth-century socialists was precisely to develop a
class consciousness in the proletariat; we see in the life
of Flora Tristan, for example, how thankless such a
task was: what she wanted for the workers had first to be
wanted without them. "But what right does one have
to want something for others?" asks the conservative,
who meanwhile regards the workingman or the native
as "a grown-up child" and who does not hesitate to dispose of the child's will. Indeed, there is nothing more
arbitrary than intervening as a stranger in a destiny which
is not ours: one of the shocking things about charity — in
the civic sense of the word — is that it is practised from
the outside, according to the caprice of the one who
distributes it and who is detached from the object. But
the cause of freedom is not that of others more than
it is mine: it is universally human. If I want the slave
to become conscious of his servitude, it is both in order
not to be a tyrant myself — for any abstention is complicity, and complicity in this case is tyranny — and in
order that new possibilities might be opened to the liberated slave and through him to all men. To want exist-

86

ence, to want to disclose the world, and to want men to be free are one and the same will.

Moreover, the oppressor is lying if he claims that the oppressed positively wants oppression; he merely abstains from not wanting it because he is unaware of even the possibility of rejection. All that an external action can propose is to put the oppressed in the presence of his freedom: then he will decide positively and freely. The fact is that he decides against oppression, and it is then that the movement of emancipation really begins. For if it is true that the cause of freedom is the cause of each one, it is also true that the urgency of liberation is not the same for all; Marx has rightly said that it is only to the oppressed that it appears as immediately necessary. As for us, we do not believe in a literal necessity but in a moral exigence; the oppressed can fulfill his freedom as a man only in revolt, since the essential characteristic of the situation against which he is rebelling is precisely its prohibiting him from any positive development; it is only in social and political struggle that his transcendence passes beyond to the infinite. And certainly the proletarrian is no more naturally a moral man than another; he can flee from his freedom, dissipate it, vegetate without desire, and give himself up to an inhuman myth; and the trick of "enlightened" capitalism is to make him forget about his concern with genuine justification, offering him, when he leaves the factory where a mechanical job absorbs his transcendence, diversions in which this transcendence ends by petering out: there you have the politics of the American employing class which catches the worker in the trap of sports, "gadgets," autos, and frigidaires. On the whole, however, he has fewer temptations of betrayal than the members of the privileged classes because the satisfying of his passions, the taste for adventure, and the satisfactions of social seriousness are denied him. And in particular, it is also possible for the bourgeois and the intellectual to use their freedom positively at the same time as they can cooperate in the struggle against oppression: their future is not barred. That is what Ponge, for example, suggests when he writes that he is producing "post-revolutionary" literature. The writer, as well as the scientist and the technician, has the possibility of realizing, before the revolution is accomplished, this re-creation of the world which should be the task of every man if freedom were no longer enchained anywhere. Whether or not it is desirable to anticipate the future, whether men have to give up the positive use of their freedom as long as the liberation of all has not yet been achieved, or whether, on the contrary, any human fulfillment serves the cause of man, is a point about which revolutionary politics itself is still hesitating. Even in the Soviet Union itself the relation between the building of the future and the present struggle seems to be defined in very different ways according to the moment and the circumstances. It is also a matter wherein each individual has to invent his solution freely. In any case, we can assert that the oppressed is more totally engaged in the struggle than those who, though at one with him in rejecting his servitude, do not experience it; but also that, on the other hand, every man is affected by this struggle in so essential a way that he can not fulfill himself morally without taking part in it.

The problem is complicated in practice by the fact that today oppression has more than one aspect: the Arabian fellah is oppressed by both the sheiks and the French and English administration; which of the two enemies is to be combatted? The interests of the French proletariat are not the same as those of the natives in the colonies: which are to be served? But here the question is political before being moral: we must end by abolishing all suppression; each one must carry on his struggle in connection with that of the other and by integrating it into the general pattern. What order should be followed? What tactics should be adopted? It is a matter of opportunity and efficiency. For each one it also depends upon his individual situation. It is possible that he may be led to sacrifice temporarily a cause whose success is subordinate to that of a cause whose defense is more urgent; on the other hand, it is possible that one may judge it necessary to maintain the tension of revolt against a situation to which one does not wish to consent at any price: thus, during the war, when Negro leaders in America were asked to drop their own claims for the sake of the general interest, Richard Wright refused; he thought that even in time of war his cause had to be defended. In any case, morality requires that the combatant be not blinded by the goal which he sets up for himself to the point of falling into the fanaticism of seriousness or passion. The cause which he serves must not lock itself up and thus create a new element of separation: through his own struggle he must seek to serve the universal cause of freedom.

At once the oppressor raises an objection: under the pretext of freedom, he says, there you go oppressing me in turn; you deprive me of *my* freedom. It is the argument which the Southern slaveholders opposed to the abolitionists, and we know that the Yankees were so imbued with the principles of an abstract democracy that they did not grant that they had the right to deny the Southern planters the freedom to own slaves; the Civil War broke out with a completely formal pretext. We smile at such scruples; yet today America still recognizes more or less implicitly that Southern whites have the freedom to lynch negroes. And it is the same sophism which is innocently displayed in the newspapers of the P. R. L. (Parti Republicain de la Liberte) and, more or less subtly, in all conservative organs. When a party promises the directing classes that it will defend their freedom, it means quite plainly that it demands that they have the freedom of exploiting the working class. A claim of this kind does not outrage us in the name of abstract justice; but a contradiction is dishonestly concealed there. For a freedom wills itself genuinely only by willing itself as an indefinite movement through the freedom of others; as soon as it withdraws into itself, it denies itself on behalf of some object which it prefers to itself: we know well enough what sort of freedom the P. R. L. demands: it is property, the feeling of possession, capital, comfort, moral security. We have to respect freedom only when it is intended for freedom, not when it strays, flees itself, and resigns itself. A freedom which is interested only in denying freedom must be denied. And it is not true that the recognition of the freedom of others limits my own freedom: to be free is not to have the power to do anything you like; it is to be able to surpass the given toward an open future; the existence of others as a freedom defines my situation and is even the condition of my own freedom. I am oppressed if I am thrown into prison, but not if I am kept from throwing my neighbor into prison.

Indeed, the oppressor himself is conscious of this sophism; he hardly dares to have recourse to it; rather than make an unvarnished demand for freedom to oppress he is more apt to present himself as the defender of certain values. It is not in his own name that he is fighting, but rather in the name of civilization, of institutions, of monuments, and of virtues which realize objectively the situation which he intends to maintain; he declares that all these things are beautiful and good in themselves; he defends a past which has assumed the icy dignity of being against an uncertain future whose values have not yet been won; this is what is well expressed by the label "conservative." As some people are curators of a museum or a collection of medals, others make themselves the curators of the given world; stressing the sacrifices that are necessarily involved in all change, they side with what has been over against what has not yet been.

It is quite certain that the surpassing of the past toward the future always demands sacrifices; to claim that in

91

destroying an old quarter in order to build new houses on its ruins one is preserving it dialectically is a play on words; no dialectic can restore the old port of Marseilles; the past as something not surpassed, in its flesh and blood presence, has completely vanished. All that a stubborn optimism can claim is that the past does not concern us in this particular and fixed form and that we have sacrificed nothing in sacrificing it; thus, many revolutionaries consider it healthy to refuse any attachment to the past and to profess to scorn monuments and traditions. A left-wing journalist who was fuming impatiently in a street of Pompeii said, "What are we doing here? We're wasting our time." This attitude is self-confirming; let us turn away from the past, and there no longer remains any trace of it in the present, or for the future; the people of the Middle Ages had so well forgotten antiquity that there was no longer anyone who even had a desire to know something about it. One can live without Greek, without Latin, without cathedrals, and without history. Yes, but there are many other things that one can live without; the tendency of man is not to reduce himself but to increase his power. To abandon the past to the night of facticity is a way of depopulating the world. I would distrust a humanism which was too indifferent to the efforts of the men of former times; if the disclosure of being achieved by our ancestors does not at all move us, why be so interested in that which is taking place today; why wish so ardently for future realizations? To assert the reign of the human is to acknowledge man in the past as well in the future. The Humanists of the

Renaissance are an example of the help to be derived by a movement of liberation from being rooted in the past; no doubt the study of Greek and Latin does not have this living force in every age; but in any case, the fact of having a past is part of the human condition; if the world behind us were bare, we would hardly be able to see anything before us but a gloomy desert. We must try, through our living projects, to turn to our own account that freedom which was undertaken in the past and to integrate it into the present world.

But on the other hand, we know that if the past concerns us, it does so not as a brute fact, but insofar as it has human signification; if this signification can be recognized only by a project which refuses the legacy of the past, then this legacy must be refused; it would be absurd to uphold against man a datum which is precious only insofar as the freedom of man is expressed in it. There is one country where the cult of the past is erected into a system more than anywhere else: it is the Portugal of today; but it is at the cost of a deliberate contempt for man. Salazar has had brand-new castles built, at great expense, on all the hills where there were ruins standing, and at Obidos he had no hesitation in appropriating for this restoration the funds that were to go to the maternity hospital, which, as a result, had to be closed; on the outskirts of Coimbre where a children's community was to be set up, he spent so much money having the different types of old Portuguese houses reproduced on a reduced scale that barely four children could be lodged in this monstrous village. Dances, songs, local festivals, and the wearing of old regional costumes are encouraged everywhere: they never open a school. Here we see, in its extreme form, the absurdity of a choice which prefers the Thing to Man from whom alone the Thing can receive its value. We may be moved by dances, songs, and regional costumes because these inventions represent the only free accomplishment which was allowed the peasants amidst the hard conditions under which they formerly lived; by means of these creations they tore themselves away from their servile work, transcended their situation, and asserted themselves as men before the beasts of burden. Wherever these festivals still exist spontaneously, where they have retained this character, they have their meaning and their value. But when they are ceremoniously reproduced for the edification of indifferent tourists, they are no more than a boring documentary, even an odious mystification. It is a sophism to want to maintain by coercion things which derive their worth from the fact that men attempted through them to escape from coercion. In like manner, all those who oppose old lace, rugs, peasant coifs, picturesque houses, regional costumes, hand-made cloth, old language, etcetera, to social evolution know very well that they are dishonest: they themselves do not much value the present reality of these things, and most of the time their lives clearly show it. To be sure, they treat those who do not recognize the unconditional value of an Alencon point as ignoramuses; but at heart they know that these objects are less precious in themselves than as the manifestation of the civilization which they repre-

94

sent. They are crying up the patience and the submission of industrious hands which were one with their needle as much as they are the lace. We also know that the Nazis made very handsome bindings and lampshades out of human skin.

Thus, oppression can in no way justify itself in the name of the content which it is defending and which it dishonestly sets up as an idol. Bound up with the subjectivity which established it, this content requires its own surpassing. One does not love the past in its living truth if he insists on preserving its hardened and mummified forms. The past is an appeal; it is an appeal toward the future which sometimes can save it only by destroying it. Even though this destruction may be a sacrifice, it would be a lie to deny it: since man wants there to be being, he can not renounce any form of being without regret. But a genuine ethics does not teach us either to sacrifice it or deny it: we must assume it.

The oppressor does not merely try to justify himself as a conserver. Often he tries to invoke future realizations; he speaks in the name of the future. Capitalism sets itself up as the regime which is most favorable to production; the colonist is the only one capable of exploiting the wealth which the native would leave fallow. Oppression tries to defend itself by its utility. But we have seen that it is one of the lies of the serious mind to attempt to give the word "useful" an absolute meaning; nothing is useful if it is not useful to man; nothing is useful to man if the latter is not in a position to define his own ends and values, if he is not free. Doubtless an oppressive regime can achieve constructions which will serve man: they will serve him only from the day that he is free to use them; as long as the reign of the oppressor lasts, none of the benefits of oppression is a real benefit. Neither in the past nor in the future can one prefer a thing to Man, who alone can establish the reason for all things.

Finally, the oppressor has a good case for showing that respect for freedom is never without difficulty, and perhaps he may even assert that one can never respect all freedoms at the same time. But that simply means that man must accept the tension of the struggle, that his liberation must actively seek to perpetuate itself, without aiming at an impossible state of equilibrium and rest; this does not mean that he ought to prefer the sleep of slavery to this incessant conquest. Whatever the problems raised for him, the setbacks that he will have to assume, and the difficulties with which he will have to struggle, he must reject oppression at any cost.

3. The Antinomies of Action

As we have seen, if the oppressor were aware of the demands of his own freedom, he himself should have to denounce oppression. But he is dishonest; in the name of the serious or of his passions, of his will for power or of his appetites, he refuses to give up his privileges. In order for a liberating action to be a thoroughly moral action, it would have to be achieved through a conversion of the oppressors: there would then be a reconciliation of all

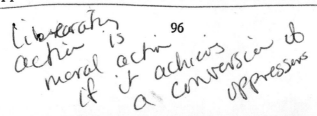

Liberation action is moral action if it achieves a conversion of oppressors

freedoms. But no one any longer dares to abandon himself today to these utopian reveries. We know only too well that we can not count upon a collective conversion. However, by virtue of the fact that the oppressors refuse to co-operate in the affirmation of freedom, they embody, in the eyes of all men of good will, the absurdity of facticity; by calling for the triumph of freedom over facticity, ethics also demands that they be suppressed; and since their subjectivity, by definition, escapes our control, it will be possible to act only on their objective presence; others will here have to be treated like things, with violence; the sad fact of the separation of men will thereby be confirmed. Thus, here is the oppressor oppressed in turn; and the men who do violence to him in their turn become masters, tyrants, and executioners: in revolting, the oppressed are metamorphosed into a blind force, a brutal fatality; the evil which divides the world is carried out in their own hearts. And doubtless it is not a question of backing out of these consequences, for the ill-will of the oppressor imposes upon each one the alternative of being the enemy of the oppressed if he is not that of their tyrant; evidently, it is necessary to choose to sacrifice the one who is an enemy of man; but the fact is that one finds himself forced to treat certain men as things in order to win the freedom of all.

A freedom which is occupied in denying freedom is itself so outrageous that the outrageousness of the violence which one practises against it is almost cancelled out: hatred, indignation, and anger (which even the Marxist cultivates, despite the cold impartiality of the doctrine) wipe out all scruples. But the oppressor would not be so strong if he did not have accomplices among the oppressed themselves; mystification is one of the forms of oppression; ignorance is a situation in which man may be enclosed as narrowly as in a prison; as we have already said, every individual may practise his freedom inside his world, but not everyone has the means of rejecting, even by doubt, the values, taboos, and prescriptions by which he is surrounded; doubtless, respectful minds take the object of their respect for their own; in this sense they are *responsible* for it, as they are responsible for their presence in the world: but they are not *guilty* if their adhesion is not a resignation of their freedom. When a young sixteen-year old Nazi died crying, "Heil Hitler!" he was not guilty, and it was not he whom we hated but his masters. The desirable thing would be to re-educate this misled youth; it would be necessary to expose the mystification and to put the men who are its victims in the presence of their freedom. But the urgency of the struggle forbids this slow labor. We are obliged to destroy not only the oppressor but also those who serve him, whether they do so out of ignorance or out of constraint.

As we have also seen, the situation of the world is so complex that one can not fight everywhere at the same time and for everyone. In order to win an urgent victory, one has to give up the idea, at least temporarily, of serving certain valid causes; one may even be brought to the point of fighting against them. Thus, during the course of the last war, no Anti-fascist could have wanted the revolts of the natives in the British Empire to be successful; on the contrary, these revolts were supported by the Fascist regimes; and yet, we can not blame those who, considering their emancipation to be the more urgent action, took advantage of the situation to obtain it. Thus, it is possible, and often it even happens, that one finds himself obliged to oppress and kill men who are pursuing goals whose validity one acknowledges himself.

But that is not the worst thing to be said for violence. It not only forces us to sacrifice the men who are in our way, but also those who are fighting on our side, and even ourselves. Since we can conquer our enemies only by acting upon their facticity, by reducing them to things, we have to make ourselves things; in this struggle in which wills are forced to confront each other through their bodies, the bodies of our allies, like those of our opponents are exposed to the same brutal hazard: they will be wounded, killed, or starved. Every war, every revolution, demands the sacrifice of a generation, of a collectivity, by those who undertake it. And even outside of periods of crisis when blood flows, the permanent possibility of violence can constitute between nations and classes a state of veiled warfare in which individuals are sacrificed in a permanent way.

Thus one finds himself in the presence of the paradox that no action can be generated for man without its being immediately generated against men. This obvious truth, which is universally known, is, however, so bitter that the first concern of a doctrine of action is ordinarily to mask this element of failure that is involved in any undertaking. The parties of oppression beg the question;

99

they deny the value of what they sacrifice in such a way that they find that they are sacrificing *nothing*. Passing dishonestly from the serious to nihilism, they set up both the unconditioned value of their end and the insignificance of the men whom they are using as instruments. High as it may be, the number of victims is always measurable; and each one taken one by one is never anything but an individual: yet, through time and space, the triumph of the cause embraces the infinite, it interests the whole collectivity. In order to deny the outrage it is enough to deny the importance of the individual, even though it be at the cost of this collectivity: *it* is everything, *he* is only a zero.

In one sense the individual, as a matter of fact, is not very much, and we can understand the misanthrope who in 1939 declared: "After all, when you look at people one by one, it doesn't seem so awful a thing to make war upon them." Reduced to pure facticity, congealed in his immanence, cut off from his future, deprived of his transcendence and of the world which that transcendence discloses, a man no longer appears as anything more than a thing among things which can be subtracted from the collectivity of other things without its leaving upon the earth any trace of its absence. Multiply this paltry existence by thousands of copies and its insignificance remains; mathematics also teaches us that zero multipled by any finite number remains zero. It is even possible that the wretchedness of each element is only further affirmed by this futile expansion. Horror is sometimes self-destructive before the photographs of the charnel-houses of Buchenwald and Dachau and of the ditches strewn with bones; it takes on the aspect of indifference; that decomposed, that animal flesh seems so essentially doomed to decay that one can no longer even regret that it has fulfilled its destiny; it is when a man is alive that his death appears to be an outrage, but a corpse has the stupid tranquillity of trees and stones: those who have done it say that it is easy to walk on a corpse and still easier to walk over a pile of corpses; and it is the same reason that accounts for the callousness described by those deportees who escaped death: through sickness, pain, hunger, and death, they no longer saw their comrades and themselves as anything more than an animal horde whose life or desires were no longer justified by anything, whose very revolts were only the agitations of animals. In order to remain capable of perceiving man through these humiliated bodies one had to be sustained by political faith, intellectual pride, or Christian charity. That is why the Nazis were so systematically relentless in casting into abjection the men they wanted to destroy: the disgust which the victims felt in regard to themselves stifled the voice of revolt and justified the executioners in their own eyes. All oppressive regimes become stronger through the degradation of the oppressed. In Algeria I have seen any number of colonists appease their conscience by the contempt in which they held the Arabs who were crushed with misery: the more miserable the latter were, the more contemptible they seemed, so much so that there was never any room for remorse. And the truth is that certain tribes in the south were so ravaged by disease

101

and famine that one could no longer feel either rebellious or hopeful regarding them; rather, one wished for the death of those unhappy creatures who have been reduced to so elemental an animality that even the maternal instict has been suppressed in them. Yet, with all this sordid resignation, there were children who played and laughed; and their smile exposed the lie of their oppressors: it was an appeal and a promise; it projected a future before the child, a man's future. If, in all oppressed countries, a child's face is so moving, it is not that the child is more moving or that he has more of a right to happiness than the others: it is that he is the living affirmation of human transcendence: he is on the watch, he is an eager hand held out to the world, he is a hope, a project. The trick of tyrants is to enclose a man in the immanence of his facticity and to try to forget that man is always, as Heidegger puts it, "infinitely more than what he would be if he were reduced to being what he is;" man is a being of the distances, a movement toward the future, a project. The tyrant asserts himself as a transcendence; he considers others as pure immanences: he thus arrogates to himself the right to treat them like cattle. We see the sophism on which his conduct is based: of the ambiguous condition which is that of all men, he retains for himself the only aspect of a transcendence which is capable of justifying itself; for the others, the contingent and unjustified aspect of immanence.

But if that kind of contempt for man is convenient, it is also dangerous; the feeling of abjection can confirm men in a hopeless resignation but can not incite them to

102

the struggle and sacrifice which is consented to with their life; this was seen in the time of the Roman decadence when men lost their zest for life and the readiness to risk it. In any case, the tyrant himself does not openly set up this contempt as a universal principle: it is the Jew, the negro, or the native whom he encloses in his immanence; with his subordinates and his soldiers he uses different language. For it is quite clear that if the individual is a pure zero, the sum of those zeros which make up the collectivity is also a zero: no undertaking has any importance, no defeat as well as no victory. In order to appeal to the devotion of his troops, the chief or the authoritarian party will utilize a truth which is the opposite of the one which sanctions their brutal oppression: namely, that the value of the individual is asserted only in his surpassing. This is one of the aspects of the doctrine of Hegel which the dictatorial regimes readily make use of. And it is a point at which fascist ideology and Marxist ideology converge. A doctrine which aims at the liberation of man evidently can not rest on a contempt for the individual; but it can propose to him no other salvation than his subordination to the collectivity. The finite is nothing if it is not its transition to the infinite; the death of an individual is not a failure if it is integrated into a project which surpasses the limits of life, the substance of this life being outside of the individual himself, in the class, in the socialist State; if the individual is taught to consent to his sacrifice, the latter is abolished as such, and the soldier who has renounced himself in favor of his cause will die joyfully; in fact, that is how the young Hitlerians died.

We know how many edifying speeches this philosophy has inspired: it is by losing oneself that one finds himself, by dying that one fulfills his life, by accepting servitude that one realizes his freedom; all leaders of men preach in this vein. And if there are any who refuse to heed this language, they are wrong, they are cowards: as such, they are worthless, they aren't worth anyone's bothering with them. The brave man dies gaily, of his own free will; the one who rejects death deserves only to die. There you have the problem elegantly resolved.

But one may ask whether this convenient solution is not self-contesting. In Hegel the individual is only an abstract moment in the History of absolute Mind. This is explained by the first intuition of the system which, identifying the real and the rational, empties the human world of its sensible thickness; if the truth of the here and now is only Space and Time, if the truth of one's cause is its passage into the other, then the attachment to the individual substance of life is evidently an error, an inadequate attitude. The essential moment of Hegelian ethics is the moment when consciousnesses recognize one another; in this operation the other is recognized as identical with me, which means that in myself it is the universal truth of my self which alone is recognized; so individuality is denied, and it can no longer reappear except on the natural and contingent plane; moral salvation will lie in my surpassing toward that other who is equal to myself and who in turn will surpass himself toward another. Hegel himself recognizes that if this passage continued indefinitely, Totality would never be achieved, the real would peter out in the same measure: one can not, without absurdity, indefinitely sacrifice each generation to the following one; human history would then be only an endless succession of negations which would never return to the positive; all action would be destruction and life would be a vain flight. We must admit that there will be a recovery of the real and that all sacrifices will find their positive form within the absolute Mind. But this does not work without some difficulty. The Mind is a subject; but *who* is a subject? After Descartes how can we ignore the fact that subjectivity radically signifies separation? And if it is admitted, at the cost of a contradiction, that *the* subject will be *the* men of the future reconciled, it must be clearly recognized that the men of today who turn out to have been the *substance* of the real, and not *subjects,* remain excluded forever from this reconciliation. Furthermore, even Hegel retreats from the idea of this motionless future; since Mind is restlessness, the dialectic of struggle and conciliation can never be stopped: the future which it envisages is not the perpetual peace of Kant but an indefinite state of war. It declares that this war will no longer appear as a temporary evil in which each individual makes a gift of himself to the State; but it is precisely at this point that there is a bit of sleight-of-hand: for *why* would he agree to this gift since the State can not be the achieving of the real, Totality recovering itself? The whole system seems like a huge mystification, since it subordinates all its moments to an end term whose coming it dares not set up; the individual renounces himself; but no reality in favor of which he can renounce himself is ever affirmed or recovered. Through all this learned dialectic we finally come back to the sophism which we exposed: if the individual is nothing, society can not be something. Take his substance away from him, and the State has no more substance; if he has nothing to sacrifice, there is nothing before him to sacrifice to. Hegelian fullness immediately passes into the nothingness of absence. And the very grandeur of that failure makes this truth shine forth: only the subject can justify his own existence; no external subject, no object, can bring him salvation from the outside. He can not be regarded as a nothing, since the consciousness of all things is within him.

Thus, nihilistic pessimism and rationalistic optimism fail in their effort to juggle away the bitter truth of sacrifice: they also eliminate all reasons for wanting it. Someone told a young invalid who wept because she had to leave her home, her occupations, and her whole past life, "Get cured. The rest has no importance." "But if nothing has any importance," she answered, "what good is it to get cured?" She was right. In order for this world to have any importance, in order for our undertaking to have a meaning and to be worthy of sacrifices, we must affirm the concrete and particular thickness of this world and the individual reality of our projects and ourselves. This is what democratic societies understand; they strive to confirm citizens in the feeling of their individual value; the whole ceremonious apparatus of baptism, marriage, and burial is the collectivity's homage to the individual; and the rites of justice seek to manifest society's respect for each of its members considered in his particularity. After or during a period of violence when men are treated like objects, one is astonished, even irritated, at seeing human life rediscover, in certain cases, a sacred character. Why those hesitations of the courts, those long drawn-out trials, since men died by the million, like animals, since the very ones being judged coldly massacred them? The reason is that once the period of crisis, in which the democracies themselves, whether they liked it or not, had to resort to blind violence, has passed, they aim to re-establish the individual within his rights; more than ever they must restore to their members the sense of their dignity, the sense of the dignity of each man, taken one by one; the soldier must become a citizen again so that the city may continue to subsist as such, may continue to deserve one's dedicating oneself to it.

But if the individual is set up as a unique and irreducible value, the word sacrifice regains all its meaning; what a man loses in renouncing his plans, his future, and his life no longer appears as a negligible thing. Even if he decides that in order to justify his life he must consent to limiting its course, even if he accepts dying, there is a wrench at the heart of this acceptance, for freedom demands both that it recover itself as an absolute and that it prolong its movement indefinitely: it is through this indefinite movement that it desires to come back to itself and to confirm itself; now, death puts an end to his drive; the hero can transcend death toward a future fulfillment, but he will not be present in that future; this must be understood if one wishes to restore to heroism

107

its true worth: it is neither natural nor easy; the hero may overcome his regret and carry out his sacrifice; the latter is none the less an absolute renunciation. The death of those to whom we are attached by particular ties will also be consented to as an individual and irreducible misfortune. A collectivist conception of man does not concede a valid existence to such sentiments as love, tenderness, and friendship; the abstract identity of individuals merely authorizes a comradeship between them by means of which each one is likened to each of the others. In marching, in choral singing, in common work and struggle, all the others appear as the same; nobody ever dies. On the contrary, if individuals recognize themselves in their differences, individual relations are established among them, and each one becomes irreplaceable for a few others. And violence does not merely provoke in the world the wrench of the sacrifice to which one has consented; it is also undergone in revolt and refusal. Even the one who desires a victory and who knows that it has to be paid for will wonder: why with *my* blood rather than with another's? Why is it my son who is dead? And we have seen that every struggle obliges us to sacrifice people whom our victory does not concern, people who, in all honesty, reject it as a cataclysm: these people will die in astonishment, anger or despair. Undergone as a misfortune, violence appears as a crime to the one who practices it. That is why Saint-Just, who believed in the individual and who knew that all authority is violence, said with somber lucidity, "No one governs innocently."

We may well assume that not all those who govern have

the courage to make such a confession; and furthermore it might be dangerous for them to make it too loudly. They try to mask the crime from themselves; at least they try to conceal it from the notice of those who submit to their law. If they can not totally deny it, they attempt to justify it. The most radical justification would be to demonstrate that it is necessary: it then ceases to be a crime, it becomes fatality. Even if an end is posited as necessary, the contingency of the means renders the chief's decisions arbitrary, and each individual suffering appears as unjustified: why this bloody revolution instead of slow reforms? And who will dare to designate the victim who is anonymously demanded by the general plan? On the contrary, if only one way shows itself to be possible, if the unrolling of history is fatal, there is no longer any place for the anguish of choice, or for regret, or for outrage; revolt can no longer surge up in any heart. This is what makes historical materialism so reassuring a doctrine; the troublesome idea of a subjective caprice or an objective chance is thereby eliminated. The thought and the voice of the directors merely reflect the fatal exigences of History. But in order that this faith be living and efficacious, it is necessary that no reflection mediatize the subjectivity of the chiefs and make it appear as such; if the chief considers that he does not simply reflect the given situation but that he is interpreting it, he becomes a prey to anguish: who am I to believe in myself? And if the soldier's eyes open, he too asks: who is he to command me? Instead of a prophet, he sees nothing more than a tyrant. That is why every authoritarian party regards thought as a danger

109

and reflection as a crime; it is by means of thought that crime appears as such in the world. This is one of the meanings of Koestler's *Darkness at Noon*. Roubatchov easily slips into confession because he feels that hesitation and doubt are the most radical, the most unpardonable of faults; they undermine the world of objectivity much more than does an act of capricious disobedience. Yet, however cruel the yoke may be, in spite of the purges, murders, and deportations, every regime has opponents: there are reflection, doubt, and contestation. And even if the opponent is in the wrong, his error brings to light a truth, namely, that there is a place in this world for error and subjectivity; whether he is right or wrong, he triumphs; he shows that the men who are in power may also be mistaken. And furthermore, the latter know it; they know that they hesitate and that their decisions are risky. The doctrine of necessity is much more a weapon than a faith; and if they use it, they do so because they know well enough that the soldier may act otherwise than he does, otherwise than the way they want him to, that he may disobey; they know well enough that he is free and that they are fettering his freedom. It is the first sacrifice that they impose upon him: in order to achieve the liberation of men he has to give up his own freedom, even his freedom of thought. In order to mask the violence, what they do is to have recourse to a new violence which even invades his mind.

Very well, replies the partisan who is sure of his aims, but this violence is useful. And the justification which he here invokes is that which, in the most general way,

110

inspires and legitimizes all action. From conservatives to revolutionaries, through idealistic and moral vocabularies or realistic and positive ones, the outrageousness of violence is excused in the name of utility. It does not much matter that the action is not fatally commanded by anterior events as long as it is called for by the proposed end; this end sets up the means which are subordinated to it; and thanks to this subordination, one can perhaps not avoid sacrifice but one can legitimize it: this is what is important to the man of action; like Saint-Just, he accepts the loss of his innocence. It is the arbitrariness of the crime that is repugnant to him more than the crime itself. If the sacrifices which have been assented to find their rational place within the enterprise, one escapes from the anguish of decision and from remorse. But one has to win out; defeat would change the murders and destruction into unjustified outrage, since they would have been carried out in vain; but victory gives meaning and utility to all the misfortunes which have helped bring it about.

Such a position would be solid and satisfactory if the word *useful* had an absolute meaning in itself; as we have seen, the characteristic of the spirit of seriousness is precisely to confer a meaning upon it by raising the Thing or the Cause to the dignity of an unconditioned end. The only problem then raised is a technical problem; the means will be chosen according to their effectiveness, their speed, and their economy; it is simply a question of measuring the relationships of the factors of time, cost, and probability of success. Furthermore, in war-time discipline spares the subordinates the problems of such calcu-

111

lations; they concern only the staff. The soldier does not call into question either the aim or the means of attaining it: he obeys without any discussion. However, what distinguishes war and politics from all other techniques is that the material that is employed is a human material. Now human efforts and lives can no more be treated as blind instruments than human work can be treated as simple merchandise; at the same time as he is a means for attaining an end, man is himself an end. The word *useful* requires a complement, and there can be only one: man himself. And the most disciplined soldier would mutiny if skillful propaganda did not persuade him that he is dedicating himself to the cause of man: to his cause.

But is the cause of Man that of each man? That is what utilitarian ethics has been striving to demonstrate since Hegel; if one wishes to give the word *useful* a universal and absolute meaning, it is always a question of reabsorbing each man into the bosom of mankind; it is said that despite the weaknesses of the flesh and that particular fear which each one experiences in the face of his particular death, the real interest of each one is mingled with the general interest. And it is true that each is bound to all; but that is precisely the ambiguity of his condition: in his surpassing toward others, each one exists absolutely as for himself; each is interested in the liberation of all, but as a separate existence engaged in his own projects. So much so that the terms "useful to Man," "useful to this man," do not overlap. Universal, absolute man exists nowhere. From this angle, we again come upon the same antinomy: the only justification of sacrifice is its utility;

but the useful is what serves Man. Thus, in order to serve some men we must do disservice to others. By what principle are we to choose between them?

It must again be called to mind that the supreme end at which man must aim is his freedom, which alone is capable of establishing the value of every end; thus, comfort, happiness, all relative goods which human projects define, will be subordinated to this absolute condition of realization. The freedom of a single man must count more than a cotton or rubber harvest; although this principle is not respected in fact, it is usually recognized theoretically. But what makes the problem so difficult is that it is a matter of choosing between the negation of one freedom or another: every war supposes a discipline, every revolution a dictatorship, every political move a certain amount of lying; action implies all forms of enslaving, from murder to mystification. Is it therefore absurd in every case? Or, in spite of everything, are we able to find, within the very outrage that it implies, reasons for wanting one thing rather than another?

One generally takes numerical considerations into account by a strange compromise which clearly shows that every action treats men both as a means and as an end, as an external object and as an inwardness; it is better to save the lives of ten men than of only one. Thus, one treats man as an end, for to set up quantity as a value is to set up the positive value of each unit; but it is setting it up as a quantifiable value, thus, as an externality. I have known a Kantian rationalist who passionately maintained that it is as inmoral to choose the death of a single man as to let ten thousand die; he was right in the sense that in each murder the outrage is total; ten thousand dead — there are never ten thousand copies of a single death; no multiplication is relevant to subjectivity. But he forgot that for the one who had the decision to make men are given, nevertheless, as objects that can be counted; it is therefore logical, though this logic implies an outrageous absurdity, to prefer the salvation of the greater number. Moreover, this position of the problem is rather abstract, for one rarely bases a choice on pure quantity. Those men among whom one hesitates have functions in society. The general who is sparing of the lives of his soldiers saves them as human material that it is useful to save for tomorrow's battles or for the reconstruction of the country; and he sometimes condemns to death thousands of civilians whose fate he is not concerned with in order to spare the lives of a hundred soldiers or ten specialists. An extreme case is the one David Rousset describes in *The Days of Our Death*: the S.S. obliged the responsible members of the concentration camps to designate which prisoners were to go to the gas chambers. The politicians agreed to assume this responsibility because they thought that they had a valid principle of selection: they protected the politicians of their party because the lives of these men who were devoted to a cause which they thought was just seemed to them to be the most useful to preserve. We know that the communists have been widely accused of this partiality; however, since one could in no way escape the

114

atrocity of these massacres, the only thing to do was to try, as far as possible, to rationalize it.

It seems as if we have hardly advanced, for we come back, in the end, to the statement that what appears as useful is to sacrifice the less useful men to the more useful. But even this shift from useful to useful will enlighten us: the complement of the word *useful* is the word *man*, but it is also the word *future*. It is man insofar as he is, according to the formula of Ponge, "the future of man." Indeed, cut off from his transcendence, reduced to the facticity of his presence, an individual is nothing; it is by his project that he fulfills himself, by the end at which he aims that he justifies himself; thus, this justification is always to come. Only the future can take the present for its own and keep it alive by surpassing it. A choice will become possible in the light of the future, which is the meaning of tomorrow because the present appears as the facticity which must be transcended toward freedom. No action is conceivable without this sovereign affirmation of the future. But we still have to agree upon what underlies this word.

4. The Present and the Future

The word *future* has two meanings corresponding to the two aspects of the ambiguous condition of man which is lack of being and which is existence; it alludes to both being and existence. When I envisage my future, I consider that movement which, prolonging my existence of today, will fulfill my present projects and will surpass

future is definite direction to a particular transcendence

them toward new ends: the future is the definite direction of a particular transcendence and it is so closely
bound up with the present that it composes with it a
single temporal form; this is the future which Heidegger
considered as a reality which is given at each moment.
But through the centuries men have dreamed of another
future in which it might be granted them to retrieve
themselves as beings in Glory, Happiness, or Justice; this
future did not prolong the present; it came down upon the
world like a cataclysm announced by signs which cut the
continuity of time: by a Messiah, by meteors, by the trum-
pets of the Last Judgment. By transporting the kingdom of
God to heaven, Christians have almost stripped it of its
temporal character, although it was promised to the believer only at the end of his life. It was the anti-Christian
humanism of the eighteenth century which brought the
myth down to earth again. Then, through the idea of progress, an idea of the future was elaborated in which its
two aspects fused: the future appeared both as the meaning of our transcendence and as the immobility of being;
it is human, terrestial, and the resting-place of things. It is
in this form that it is hesitantly reflected in the systems of
Hegel and of Comte. It is in this form that it is so often
invoked today as a unity of the World or as a finished
socialist State. In both cases the Future appears as both
the infinite and as Totality, as number and as unity of
conciliation; it is the abolition of the negative, it is ful-
ness, happiness. One might surmise that any sacrifice already made might be claimed in its name. However great
the quantity of men sacrificed today, the quantity that

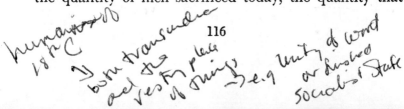

will profit by their sacrifice is infinitely greater; on the other hand, in the face of the positivity of the future, the present is only the negative which must be eliminated as such: only by dedicating itself to this positivity can the negative henceforth return to the positive. The present is the transitory existence which is made in order to be abolished: it retrieves itself only by transcending itself toward the permanence of future being; it is only as an instrument, as a means, it is only by its efficacity with regard to the coming of the future that the present is validly realized: reduced to itself it is nothing, one may dispose of it as he pleases. That is the ultimate meaning of the formula: the end justifies the means: all means are authorized by their very indifference. Thus, some serenely think that the present oppression has no importance if, through it, the World can be fulfilled as such: then, within the harmonious equilibrium of work and wealth, oppression will be wiped out by itself. Others serenely think that the present dictatorship of a party with its lies and violence has no importance if, by means of it, the socialist State is realized: arbitrariness and crime will then disappear forever from the face of the earth. And still others think more sloppily that the shilly-shallyings and the compromises have no importance since the future will turn out well and, in some way or other, will muddle along into victory. Those who project themselves toward a Future-Thing and submerge their freedom in it find the tranquillity of the serious.

However, we have seen that, despite the requirements of his system, even Hegel does not dare delude himself with the idea of a stationary future; he admits that, mind being restlessness, the struggle will never cease. Marx did not consider the coming of the socialist state as an absolute result, but as the end of a pre-history on the basis of which real history begins. However, it would be sufficient, in order for the myth of the future to be valid, for this history to be conceivable as a harmonious development where reconciled men would fulfill themselves as a pure positivity; but this dream is not permitted since man is originally a negativity. No social upheaval, no moral conversion can eliminate this lack which is in his heart; it is by making himself a lack of being that man exists, and positive existence is this lack assumed but not eliminated; we can not establish upon existence an abstract wisdom which, turning itself away from being, would aim at only the harmony itself of the existants: for it is then the absolute silence of the in-itself which would close up around this negation of negativity; without this particular movement which thrusts him toward the future man would not exist. But then one can not imagine any reconciliation of transcendences: they do not have the indifferent docility of a pure abstraction; they are concrete and concretely compete with others for being. The world which they reveal is a battle-field where there is no neutral ground and which cannot be divided up into parcels: for each individual project is asserted through the world as a whole. The fundamental ambiguity of the human condition will always open up to men the possibility of opposing choices; there will always be within them the desire to be that being of whom

the fundamental ambiguity of the h. condition will always up to men the possibility of opposing choice

they have made themselves a lack, the flight from the anguish of freedom; the plane of hell, of struggle, will never be eliminated; freedom will never be given; it will always have to be won: that is what Trotsky was saying when he envisaged the future as a permanent revolution. Thus, there is a fallacy hidden in that abuse of language which all parties make use of today to justify their politics when they declare that the world is still at war. If one means by that that the struggle is not over, that the world is a prey to opposed interests which affront each other violently, he is speaking the truth; but he also means that such a situation is abnormal and calls for abnormal behavior; the politics that it involves can impugn every moral principle, since it has only a provisional form: later on we shall act in accordance with truth and justice. To the idea of present war there is opposed that of a future peace when man will again find, along with a stable situation, the possibility of a morality. But the truth is that if division and violence define war, the world has always been at war and always will be; if man is waiting for universal peace in order to establish his existence validly, he will wait indefinitely: there will never be any *other* future.

It is possible that some may challenge this assertion as being based upon debatable ontological presuppositions; it should at least be recognized that this harmonious future is only an uncertain dream and that in any case it is not ours. Our hold on the future is limited; the movement of expansion of existence requires that we strive at every moment to amplify it; but where it stops our fu-

119

ture stops too; beyond, there is nothing more because nothing more is disclosed. From that formless night we can draw no justification of our acts, it condemns them with the same indifference; wiping out today's errors and defeats, it will also wipe out its triumphs; it can be chaos or death as well as paradise: perhaps men will one day return to barbarism, perhaps one day the earth will no longer be anything but an icy planet. In this perspective all moments are lost in the indistinctness of nothingness and being. Man ought not entrust the care of his salvation to this uncertain and foreign future: it is up to him to assure it within his own existence; this existence is conceivable, as we have said, only as an affirmation of the future, but of a human future, a finite future.

It is difficult today to safeguard this sense of finiteness. The Greek cities and the Roman republic were able to will themselves in their finiteness because the infinite which invested them was for them only darkness; they died because of this ignorance, but they also lived by it. Today, however, we are having a hard time living because we are so bent on outwitting death. We are aware that the whole world is interested in each of our undertakings and this spatial enlargement of our projects also governs their temporal dimension; by a paradoxical symmetry, whereas an individual accords great value to one day of his life, and a city to one year, the interests of the World are computed in centuries; the greater the human density that one envisages, the more the viewpoint of externality wins over that of internality, and the idea of externality carries with it that of quantity. Thus, the scales of measurement have changed; space and time have expanded about us: today it is a small matter that a million men and a century seem to us only a provisional moment; yet, the individual is not touched by this transformation, his life keeps the same rhythm, his death does not retreat before him; he extends his control of the world by instruments which enable him to devour distances and to multiply the output of his effort in time; but he is always only one. However, instead of accepting his limits, he tries to do away with them. He aspires to act upon everything and by knowing everything. Throughout the eighteenth and nineteenth centuries there developed the dream of a universal science which, manifesting the solidarity of the parts of the whole also admitted a universal power; it was a dream "dreamed by reason," as Valery puts it, but which was none the less hollow, like all dreams. For a scientist who would aspire to know everything about a phenomenon would dissolve it within the totality; and a man who would aspire to act upon the totality of the Universe would see the meaning of all action vanish. Just as the infinity spread out before my gaze contracts above my head into a blue ceiling, so my transcendence heaps up in the distance the opaque thickness of the future; but between sky and earth there is a perceptional field with its forms and colors; and it is in the interval which separates me today from an unforeseeable future that there are meanings and ends toward which to direct my acts. As soon as one introduces the presence of the finite individual into the world, a presence without which there is no world, finite forms stand out through time and space. And in reverse, though a landscape is not only a transition but a particular object, an event is not only a passage but a particular reality. If one denies with Hegel the concrete thickness of the here and now in favor of universal space-time, if one denies the separate consciousness in favor of Mind, one misses with Hegel the truth of the world.

It is no more necessary to regard History as a rational totality than to regard the Universe as such. Man, mankind, the universe, and history are, in Sartre's expression, "detotalized totalities," that is, separation does not exclude relation, nor vice-versa. Society exists only by means of the existence of particular individuals; likewise, human adventures stand out against the background of time, each finite to each, though they are all open to the infinity of the future and their individual forms thereby imply each other without destroying each other. A conception of this kind does not contradict that of a historical unintelligibility; for it is not true that the mind has to choose between the contingent absurdity of the discontinuous and the rationalistic necessity of the continuous; on the contrary, it is part of its function to make a multiplicity of coherent ensembles stand out against the unique background of the world and, inversely, to comprehend these ensembles in the perspective of an ideal unity of the world. Without raising the question of historical comprehension and causality it is enough to recognize the presence of intelligible sequences within temporal forms so that forecasts and consequently action may be possible. In fact, whatever may be the philosophy we adhere to, whether our uncertainty manifests an objective and fundamental contingency or whether it expresses our subjective ignorance in the face of a rigorous necessity, the practical attitude remains the same; we must decide upon the opportuneness of an act and attempt to measure its effectiveness without knowing all the factors that are present. Just as the scientist, in order to know a phenomenon, does not wait for the light of completed knowledge to break upon it; on the contrary, in illuminating the phenomenon, he helps establish the knowledge: in like manner, the man of action, in order to make a decision, will not wait for a perfect knowledge to prove to him the necessity of a certain choice; he must first choose and thus help fashion history. A choice of this kind is no more arbitrary than a hypothesis; it excludes neither reflection nor even method; but it is also free, and it implies risks that must be assumed as such. The movement of the mind, whether it be called thought or will, always starts up in the darkness. And at bottom it matters very little, practically speaking, whether there is a Science of history or not, since this Science can come to light only at the end of the future and since at each particular moment we must, in any case, maneuver in a state of doubt. The communists themselves admit that it is subjectively possible for them to be mistaken despite the strict dialectic of History. The latter is not revealed to them today in its finished form; they are obliged to foresee its development, and this foresight may be erroneous. Thus, from the political and tactical point of view there will be no difference between a doctrine of pure dialectical necessity and a doctrine which leaves room for contingency; the difference is of a moral order. For, in the first case one admits a retrieval of each moment in the future, and thus one does not aspire to justify it by itself; in the second case, each undertaking, involving only a finite future, must be lived in its finiteness and considered as an absolute which no unknown time will ever succeed in saving. In fact, the one who asserts the unity of history also recognizes that distinct ensembles stand out within it; and the one who emphasizes the particularity of these ensembles admits that they all project against a single horizon; just as for all there exist both individuals and a collectivity; the affirmation of the collectivity over against the individual is opposed, not on the plane of fact, but on the moral plane, to the assertion of a collectivity of individuals each existing for himself. The case is the same in what concerns time and its moments, and just as we believe that by denying each individual one by one, one eliminates the collectivity, we think that if man gives himself up to an indefinite pursuit of the future he will lose his existence without ever recovering it; he then resembles a madman who runs after his shadow. The means, it is said, will be justified by the end; but it is the means which define it, and if it is contradicted at the moment that it is set up, the whole enterprise sinks into absurdity. In this way the attitude of England in regard to Spain, Greece, and Palestine is defended with the pretext that she must take up position against the Russian menace in order to save, along with her own existence, her civilization and the values of democracy; but a de-

124

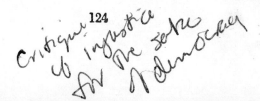

mocracy which defends itself only by acts of oppression equivalent to those of authoritarian regimes, is precisely denying all these values; whatever the virtues of a civilization may be, it immediately belies them if it buys them by means of injustice and tyranny. Inversely, if the justifying end is thrown ahead to the farthermost end of a mythical future, it is no longer a reflection upon the means; being nearer and clearer, the means itself becomes the goal aimed at; it blocks the horizon without, however, being deliberately wanted. The triumph of Russia is proposed as a means of liberating the international proletariat; but has it not become an absolute end for all Stalinists? The end justifies the means only if it remains present, if it is completely disclosed in the course of the present enterprise.

And as a matter of fact, if it is true that men seek in the future a guarantee of their success, a negation of their failures, it is true that they also feel the need of denying the indefinite flight of time and of holding their present between their hands. Existence must be asserted in the present if one does not want all life to be defined as an escape toward nothingness. That is the reason societies institute festivals whose role is to stop the movement of transcendence, to set up the end as an end. The hours following the liberation of Paris, for example, were an immense collective festival exalting the happy and absolute end of that particular history which was precisely the occupation of Paris. There were at the moment worried spirits who were already surpassing the present toward future difficulties; they refused to rejoice under the

125

pretext that new problems were going to come up immediately; but this ill-humor was met with only among those who had very slight wish to see the Germans defeated. All those who had made this combat their combat, even if only by the sincerity of their hopes, also regarded the victory as an absolute victory, whatever the future might be. Nobody was so naive as not to know that unhappiness would soon find other forms; but this particular unhappiness was wiped off the earth, absolutely. That is the modern meaning of the festival, private as well as public. Existence attempts in the festival to confirm itself positively as existence. That is why, as Bataille has shown, it is characterized by destruction; the ethics of being is the ethics of saving: by storing up, one aims at the stationary plenitude of the in-itself, existence, on the contrary, is consumption; it makes itself only by destroying; the festival carries out this negative movement in order to indicate clearly its independence in relationship to the thing: one eats, drinks, lights fires, breaks things, and spends time and money; one spends them for nothing. The spending is also a matter of establishing a communication of the existants, for it is by the movement of recognition which goes from one to the other that existence is confirmed; in songs, laughter, dances, eroticism, and drunkenness one seeks both an exaltation of the moment and a complicity with other men. But the tension of existence realized as a pure negativity can not maintain itself for long; it must be immediately engaged in a new undertaking, it must dash off toward the future. The moment of detachment, the pure affirmation of the subjective present are only abstractions; the joy becomes exhausted, drunkenness subsides into fatigue, and one finds himself with his hands empty because one can never possess the present: that is what gives festivals their pathetic and deceptive character. One of art's roles is to fix this passionate assertion of existence in a more durable way: the festival is at the origin of the theatre, music, the dance, and poetry. In telling a story, in depicting it, one makes it exist in its particularity·with its beginning and its end, its glory or its shame; and this is the way it actually must be lived. <u>In the festival, in art, men express their need to feel that they exist absolutely.</u> They must really fulfill this wish. What stops them is that as soon as they give the word "end" its double meaning of goal and fulfillment they clearly perceive this ambiguity of their condition, which is the most fundamental of all: that every living movement is a sliding toward death. But if they are willing to look it in the face they also discover that every movement toward death is life. In the past people cried out, "The king is dead, long live the king;" thus the present must die so that it may live; existence must not deny this death which it carries in its heart; it must assert itself as an absolute in its very finiteness; <u>man fulfills himself within the transitory or not at all.</u> He must regard his undertakings as <u>finite</u> and will them absolutely.

It is obvious that this finiteness is not that of the pure instant; we have said that the future was the meaning and the substance of all action; the limits can not be marked out *a priori*; there are projects which define the

127

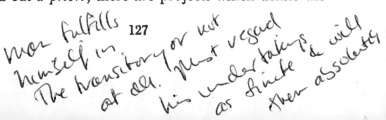

future of a day or of an hour; and there are others which are inserted into structures capable of being developed through one, two, or several centuries, and thereby they have a concrete hold on one or two or several centuries. When one fights for the emancipation of oppressed natives, or the socialist revolution, he is obviously aiming at a long range goal; and he is still aiming at it concretely, beyond his own death, through the movement, the league, the institutions, or the party that he has helped set up. What we maintain is that one must not expect that this goal be justified as a point of departure of a new future; insofar as we no longer have a hold on the time which will flow beyond its coming, we must not expect anything of that time for which we have worked; other men will have to live its joys and sorrows. As for us, the goal must be considered as an end; we have to justify it on the basis of our freedom which has projected it, by the ensemble of the movement which ends in its fulfillment. The tasks we have set up for ourselves and which, though exceeding the limits of our lives, are ours, must find their meaning in themselves and not in a mythical Historical end.

But then, if we reject the idea of a future-myth in order to retain only that of a living and finite future, one which delimits transitory forms, we have not removed the antinomy of action; the present sacrifices and failures no longer seem compensated for in any point of time. And utility can no longer be defined absolutely. Thus, are we not ending by condemning action as criminal and absurd though at the same time condemning man to action?

5. Ambiguity

The notion of ambiguity must not be confused with that of absurdity. To declare that existence is absurd is to deny that it can ever be given a meaning; to say that it is ambiguous is to assert that its meaning is never fixed, that it must be constantly won. Absurdity challenges every ethics; but also the finished rationalization of the real would leave no room for ethics; it is because man's condition is ambiguous that he seeks, through failure and outrageousness, to save his existence. Thus, to say that action has to be lived in its truth, that is, in the consciousness of the antinomies which it involves, does not mean that one has to renounce it. In *Plutarch Lied* Pierrefeu rightly says that in war there is no victory which can not be regarded as unsuccessful, for the objective which one aims at is the total annihilation of the enemy and this result is never attained; yet there are wars which are won and wars which are lost. So is it with any activity; failure and success are two aspects of reality which at the start are not perceptible. That is what makes criticism so easy and art so difficult: the critic is always in a good position to show the limits that every artist gives himself in choosing himself; painting is not given completely either in Giotto or Titian or Cezanne; it is sought through the centuries and is never finished; a painting in which all pictorial problems are resolved is really inconceivable; painting itself is this movement toward its own reality; it is not the vain displacement of a millstone turning in the void; it concretizes itself on each canvas as an absolute existence. Art and science do not establish themselves despite failure but through it; which does not prevent there being truths and errors, masterpieces and lemons, depending upon whether the discovery or the painting has or has not known how to win the adherence of human consciousnesses; this amounts to saying that failure, always ineluctable, is in certain cases spared and in others not.

It is interesting to pursue this comparison; not that we are likening action to a work of art or a scientific theory, but because in any case human transcendence must cope with the same problem: it has to found itself, though it is prohibited from ever fulfilling itself. Now, we know that neither science nor art ever leaves it up to the future to justify its present existence. In no age does art consider itself as something which is paving the way for Art: so-called archaic art prepares for classicism only in the eyes of archaeologists; the sculptor who fashioned the Korai of Athens rightfully thought that he was producing a finished work of art; in no age has science considered itself as partial and lacunary; without believing itself to be definitive, it has however, always wanted to be a total expression of the world, and it is in its totality that in each age it again raises the question of its own validity. There we have an example of how man must, in any event, assume his finiteness: not by treating his existence as transitory or relative but by reflecting the infinite within it, that is, by treating it as absolute. There is an art only because at every moment art has willed itself absolutely; likewise there is a liberation of man only

Man must assume his finiteness not by treating his existence as transitory or relative but by reflecting the infinite w/in it, by treating it as absolute.

if, in aiming at itself, freedom is achieved absolutely in the very fact of aiming at itself. This requires that each action be considered as a finished form whose different moments, instead of fleeing toward the future in order to find there their justification, reflect and confirm one another so well that there is no longer a sharp separation between present and future, between means and ends.

But if these moments constitute a unity, there must be no contradiction among them. Since the liberation aimed at is not a *thing* situated in an unfamiliar time, but a movement which realizes itself by tending to conquer, it can not attain itself if it denies itself at the start; action can not seek to fulfill itself by means which would destroy its very meaning. So much so that in certain situations there will be no other issue for man than rejection. In what is called political realism there is no room for rejection because the present is considered as transitory; there is rejection only if man lays claim in the present to his existence as an absolute value; then he must absolutely reject what would deny this value. Today, more or less consciously in the name of such an ethics, we condemn a magistrate who handed over a communist to save ten hostages and along with him all the Vichyites who were trying "to make the best of things:" it was not a matter of rationalizing the present such as it was imposed by the German occupation, but of rejecting it unconditionally. The resistance did not aspire to a positive effectiveness; it was a negation, a revolt, a martyrdom; and in this negative movement freedom was positively and absolutely confirmed.

131

In one sense the negative attitude is easy; the rejected object is given unequivocally and unequivocally defines the revolt that one opposes to it; thus, all French antifascists were united during the occupation by their common resistance to a single oppressor. The return to the positive encounters many more obstacles, as we have well seen in France where divisions and hatreds were revived at the same time as were the parties. In the moment of rejection, the antinomy of action is removed, and means and end meet; freedom immediately sets itself up as its own goal and fulfills itself by so doing. But the antinomy reappears as soon as freedom again gives itself ends which are far off in the future; then, through the resistances of the given, divergent means offer themselves and certain ones come to be seen as contrary to their ends. It has often been observed that revolt alone is pure. Every construction implies the outrage of dictatorship, of violence. This is the theme, among others, of Koestler's *Gladiators*. Those who, like this symbolic *Spartacus*, do not want to retreat from the outrage and resign themselves to impotence, usually seek refuge in the values of seriousness. That is why, among individuals as well as collectivities, the negative moment is often the most genuine. Goethe, Barres, and Aragon, disdainful or rebellious in their romantic youth, shattered old conformisms and thereby proposed a real, though incomplete, liberation. But what happened later on? Goethe became a servant of the state, Barres of nationalism, and Aragon of Stalinist conformism. We know how the seriousness of the Catholic Church was substituted for the Christian spirit, which was

132

a rejection of dead Law, a subjective rapport of the individual with God through faith and charity; the Reformation was a revolt of subjectivity, but Protestantism in turn changed into an objective moralism in which the seriousness of works replaced the restlessness of faith. As for revolutionary humanism, it accepts only rarely the tension of permanent liberation; it has created a Church where salvation is bought by membership in a party as it is bought elsewhere by baptism and indulgences. We have seen that this recourse to the serious is a lie; it entails the sacrifice of man to the Thing, of freedom to the Cause. In order for the return to the positive to be genuine it must involve negativity, it must not conceal the antinomies between means and end, present and future; they must be lived in a permanent tension; one must retreat from neither the outrage of violence nor deny it, or, which amounts to the same thing, assume it lightly. Kierkegaard has said that what distinguishes the pharisee from the genuinely moral man is that the former considers his anguish as a sure sign of his virtue; from the fact that he asks himself, "Am I Abraham?" he concludes, "I am Abraham;" but morality resides in the painfulness of an indefinite questioning. The problem which we are posing is not the same as that of Kierkegaard; the important thing to us is to know whether, in given conditions, Isaac must be killed or not. But we also think that what distinguishes the tyrant from the man of good will is that the first rests in the certainty of his aims, whereas the second keeps asking himself, "Am I really working for the liberation of men? Isn't this

133

end contested by the sacrifices through which I aim at it?" In setting up its ends, freedom must put them in parentheses, confront them at each moment with that absolute end which it itself constitutes, and contest, in its own name, the means it uses to win itself.

It will be said that these considerations remain quite abstract. What must be done, practically? Which action is good? Which is bad? To ask such a question is also to fall into a naive abstraction. We don't ask the physicist, "Which hypotheses are true?" Nor the artist, "By what procedures does one produce a work whose beauty is guaranteed?" Ethics does not furnish recipes any more than do science and art. One can merely propose methods. Thus, in science the fundamental problem is to make the idea adequate to its content and the law adequate to the facts; the logician finds that in the case where the pressure of the given fact bursts the concept which serves to comprehend it, one is obliged to invent another concept; but he can not define *a priori* the moment of invention, still less foresee it. Analogously, one may say that in the case where the content of the action falsifies its meaning, one must modify not the meaning, which is here willed absolutely, but the content itself; however, it is impossible to determine this relationship between meaning and content abstractly and universally: there must be a trial and decision in each case. But likewise just as the physicist finds it profitable to reflect on the conditions of scientific invention and the artist on those of artistic creation without expecting any ready-made solutions to come from these reflections, it is useful for the man of action to find out under what conditions his undertakings are valid. We

134

are going to see that on this basis new perspectives are disclosed.

In the first place, it seems to us that the individual as such is one of the ends at which our action must aim. Here we are at one with the point of view of Christian charity, the Epicurean cult of friendship, and Kantian moralism which treats each man as an end. He interests us not merely as a member of a class, a nation, or a collectivity, but as an individual man. This distinguishes us from the systematic politician who cares only about collective destinies; and probably a tramp enjoying his bottle of wine, or a child playing with a balloon, or a Neapolitan lazzarone loafing in the sun in no way helps in the liberation of man; that is why the abstract will of the revolutionary scorns the concrete benevolence which occupies itself in satisfying desires which have no morrow. However, it must not be forgotten that there is a concrete bond between freedom and existence; to will man free is to will there to *be* being, it is to will the disclosure of being in the joy of existence; in order for the idea of liberation to have a concrete meaning, the joy of existence must be asserted in each one, at every instant; the movement toward freedom assumes its real, flesh and blood figure in the world by thickening into pleasure, into happiness. If the satisfaction of an old man drinking a glass of wine counts for nothing, then production and wealth are only hollow myths; they have meaning only if they are capable of being retrieved in individual and living joy. The saving of time and the conquest of leisure have no meaning if we are not moved by the laugh of a child at play. If we

135

do not love life on our own account and through others, it is futile to seek to justify it in any way.

However, politics is right in rejecting benevolence to the extent that the latter thoughtlessly sacrifices the future to the present. The ambiguity of freedom, which very often is occupied only in fleeing from itself, introduces a difficult equivocation into relationships with each individual taken one by one. Just what is meant by the expression "to love others"? What is meant by taking them as ends? In any event, it is evident that we are not going to decide to fulfill the will of every man. There are cases where a man positively wants evil, that is, the enslavement of other men, and he must then be fought. It also happens that, without harming anyone, he flees from his own freedom, seeking passionately and alone to attain the being which constantly eludes him. If he asks for our help, are we to give it to him? We blame a man who helps a drug addict intoxicate himself or a desperate man commit suicide, for we think that rash behavior of this sort is an attempt of the individual against his own freedom; he must be made aware of his error and put in the presence of the real demands of his freedom. Well and good. But what if he persists? Must we then use violence? There again the serious man busies himself dodging the problem; the values of life, of health, and of moral conformism being set up, one does not hesitate to impose them on others. But we know that this pharisaism can cause the worst disasters: lacking drugs, the addict may kill himself. It is no more necessary to serve an abstract ethics obstinately than to yield without due consideration to impulses of pity or generosity; violence is justified only if it opens concrete possibilities to the freedom which I am trying to save; by practising it I am willy-nilly assuming an engagement in relation to others and to myself; a man whom I snatch from the death which he had chosen has the right to come and ask me for means and reasons for living; the tyranny practised against an invalid can be justified only by his getting better; whatever the purity of the intention which animates me, any dictatorship is a fault for which I have to get myself pardoned. Besides, I am in no position to make decisions of this sort indiscriminately; the example of the unknown person who throws himself in to the Seine and whom I hesitate whether or not to fish out is quite abstract; in the absence of a concrete bond with this desperate person my choice will never be anything but a contingent facticity. If I find myself in a position to do violence to a child, or to a melancholic, sick, or distraught person the reason is that I also find myself charged with his upbringing, his happiness, and his health: I am a parent, a teacher, a nurse, a doctor, or a friend. . . So, by a tacit agreement, by the very fact that I am solicited, the strictness of my decision is accepted or even desired; the more seriously I accept my responsibilities, the more justified it is. That is why love authorizes severities which are not granted to indifference. What makes the problem so complex is that, on the one hand, one must not make himself an accomplice of that flight from freedom that is found in heedlessness, caprice, mania, and passion, and that, on the other hand, it is the abortive movement of man toward being which is his very existence, it is through

137

the failure which he has assumed that he asserts himself as a freedom. To want to prohibit a man from error is to forbid him to fulfill his own existence, it is to deprive him of life. At the beginning of Claudel's *The Satin Shoe,* the husband of Dona Prouheze, the Judge, the Just, as the author regards him, explains that every plant needs a gardener in order to grow and that he is the one whom heaven has destined for his young wife; beside the fact that we are shocked by the arrogance of such a thought (for how does he know that he is this enlightened gardener? Isn't he merely a jealous husband?) this likening of a soul to a plant is not acceptable; for, as Kant would say, the value of an act lies not in its *conformity* to an external model, but in its internal truth. We object to the inquisitors who want to create faith and virtue from without; we object to all forms of fascism which seek to fashion the happiness of man from without; and also the paternalism which thinks that it has done something for man by prohibiting him from certain possibilities of temptation, whereas what is necessary is to give him reasons for resisting it.

Thus, violence is not immediately justified when it opposes willful acts which one considers perverted; it becomes inadmissible if it uses the pretext of ignorance to deny a freedom which, as we have seen, can be practised within ignorance itself. Let the "enlightened elites" strive to change the situation of the child, the illiterate, the primitive crushed beneath his superstitions; that is one of their most urgent tasks; but in this very effort they must respect a freedom which, like theirs, is absolute. They

Violence is not immediately justified when it opposes willful acts it considers perverted.

are always opposed, for example, to the extension of universal suffrage by adducing the incompetence of the masses, of women, of the natives in the colonies; but this forgetting that man always has to decide by himself in the darkness, that he must want beyond what he knows. If infinite knowledge were necessary (even supposing that it were conceivable), then the colonial administrator himself would not have the right to freedom; he is much further from perfect knowledge than the most backward savage is from him. Actually, to vote is not to govern; and to govern is not merely to maneuver; there is an ambiguity today, and particularly in France, because we think that we are not the master of our destiny; we no longer hope to help make history, we are resigned to submitting to it; all that our internal politics does is reflect the play of external forces, no party hopes to determine the fate of the country but merely to foresee the future which is being prepared in the world by foreign powers and to use, as best we can, the bit of indetermination which still escapes their foresight. Drawn along by this tactical realism, the citizens themselves no longer consider the vote as the assertion of their will but as a maneuver, whether one adheres completely to the maneuvering of a party or whether one invents his own strategy; the electors consider themselves not as men who are consulted about a particular point but as forces which are numbered and which are ordered about with a view to distant ends. And that is probably why the French, who formerly were so eager to declare their opinions, take no further interest in an act which has become a disheartening strategy. So, the fact is that if it is necessary not to vote but to measure the weight of one's vote, this calculation requires such extensive information and such a sureness of foresight that only a specialized technician can have the boldness to express an opinion. But that is one of the abuses whereby the whole meaning of democracy is lost; the logical conclusion of this would be to suppress the vote. The vote should really be the expression of a concrete will, the choice of a representative capable of defending, within the general framework of the country and the world, the particular interests of his electors. The ignorant and the outcast also has interests to defend; he alone is "competent" to decide upon his hopes and his trust. By a sophism which leans upon the dishonesty of the serious, one does not merely argue about his formal impotence to choose, but one draws arguments from the content of his choice. I recall, among others, the naivete of a right-thinking young girl who said, "The vote for women is all well and good in principle, only, if women get the vote, they'll all vote red." With like impudence it is almost unanimously stated today in France that if the natives of the French Union were given the rights of self-determination, they would live quietly in their villages without doing anything, which would be harmful to the higher interests of the Economy. And doubtless the state of stagnation in which they choose to live is not that which a man can wish for another man; it is desirable to open new possibilities to the indolent negroes so that the interests of the Economy may one day merge with theirs. But for the time being, they are left to vegetate in the sort of sit-

140

uation where their freedom can merely be negative: the best thing they can desire is not to tire themselves, not to suffer, and not to work; and even this freedom is denied them. It is the most consummate and inacceptable form of oppression.

However, the "enlightened elite" objects, one does not let a child dispose of himself, one does not permit him to vote. This is another sophism. To the extent that woman or the happy or resigned slave lives in the infantile world of ready-made values, calling them "an eternal child" or "a grown-up child" has some meaning, but the analogy is only partial. Childhood is a particular sort of situation: it is a natural situation whose limits are not created by other men and which is thereby not comparable to a situation of oppression; it is a situation which is common to all men and which is temporary for all; therefore, it does not represent a limit which cuts off the individual from his possibilities, but, on the contrary, the moment of a development in which new possibilities are won. The child is ignorant because he has not yet had the time to acquire knowledge, not because this time has been refused him. To treat him as a child is not to bar him from the future but to open it to him; he needs to be taken in hand, he invites authority, it is the form which the resistance of facticity, through which all liberation is brought about, takes for him. And on the other hand, even in this situation the child has a right to his freedom and must be respected as a human person. What gives *Emile* its value is the brilliance with which Rousseau asserts this principle. There is a very annoying naturalistic optimism in *Emile;*

in the rearing of the child, as in any relationship with others, the ambiguity of freedom implies the outrage of violence; in a sense, all education is a failure. But Rousseau is right in refusing to allow childhood to be oppressed. And in practice raising a child as one cultivates a plant which one does not consult about its needs is very different from considering it as a freedom to whom the future must be opened.

Thus, we can set up point number one: the good of an individual or a group of individuals requires that it be taken as an absolute end of our action; but we are not authorized to decide upon this end *a priori*. The fact is that no behavior is ever authorized to begin with, and one of the concrete consequences of existentialist ethics is the rejection of all the previous justifications which might be drawn from the civilization, the age, and the culture; it is the rejection of every principle of authority. To put it positively, the precept will be to treat the other (to the extent that he is the only one concerned, which is the moment that we are considering at present) as a freedom so that his end may be freedom; in using this conducting-wire one will have to incur the risk, in each case, of inventing an original solution. Out of disappointment in love a young girl takes an overdose of pheno-barbital; in the morning friends find her dying, they call a doctor, she is saved; later on she becomes a happy mother of a family; her friends were right in considering her suicide as a hasty and heedless act and in putting her into a position to reject it or return to it freely. But in asylums one sees melancholic patients who have tried to commit suicide twenty times, who devote their freedom to seeking the means of escaping their jailers and of putting an end to their intolerable anguish; the doctor who gives them a friendly pat on the shoulder is their tyrant and their torturer. A friend who is intoxicated by alcohol or drugs asks me for money so that he can go and buy the poison that is necessary to him; I urge him to get cured, I take him to a doctor, I try to help him live; insofar as there is a chance of my being successful, I am acting correctly in refusing him the sum he asks for. But if circumstances prohibit me from doing anything to change the situation in which he is struggling, all I can do is give in; a deprivation of a few hours will do nothing but exasperate his torments uselessly; and he may have recourse to extreme means to get what I do not give him. That is also the problem touched on by Ibsen in *The Wild Duck*. An individual lives in a situation of falsehood; the falsehood is violence, tyranny: shall I tell the truth in order to free the victim? It would first be necessary to create a situation of such a kind that the truth might be bearable and that, though losing his illusions, the deluded individual might again find about him reasons for hoping. What makes the problem more complex is that the freedom of one man almost always concerns that of other individuals. Here is a married couple who persist in living in a hovel; if one does not succeed in giving them the desire to live in a more healthful dwelling, they must be allowed to follow their preferences; but the situation changes if they have children; the freedom of the parents would be the ruin of their sons, and as freedom and the future are on the

143

side of the latter, these are the ones who must first be taken into account. The Other is multiple, and on the basis of this new questions arise.

One might first wonder for whom we are seeking freedom and happiness. When raised in this way, the problem is abstract; the answer will, therefore, be arbitrary, and the arbitrary always involves outrage. It is not entirely the fault of the district social-worker if she is apt to be odious; because, her money and time being limited, she hesitates before distributing it to this one or that one, she appears to others as a pure externality, a blind facticity. Contrary to the formal strictness of Kantianism for whom the more abstract the act is the more virtuous it is, generosity seems to us to be better grounded and therefore more valid the less distinction there is between the other and ourself and the more we fulfill ourself in taking the other as an end. That is what happens if I am engaged in relation to others. The Stoics impugned the ties of family, friendship, and nationality so that they recognized only the universal form of man. But man is man only through situations whose particularity is precisely a universal fact. There are men who expect help from certain men and not from others, and these expectations define privileged lines of action. It is fitting that the negro fight for the negro, the Jew for the Jew, the proletarian for the proletarian, and the Spaniard in Spain. But the assertion of these particular solidarities must not contradict the will for universal solidarity and each finite undertaking must also be open on the totality of men.

144

But it is then that we find in concrete form the conflicts which we have described abstractly; for the cause of freedom can triumph only through particular sacrifices. And certainly there are hierarchies among the goods desired by men: one will not hesitate to sacrifice the comfort, luxury, and leisure of certain men to assure the liberation of certain others; but when it is a question of choosing among freedoms, how shall we decide?

Let us repeat, one can only indicate a method here. The first point is always to consider what genuine human interest fills the abstract form which one proposes as the action's end. Politics always puts forward Ideas: Nation, Empire, Union, Economy, etc. But none of these forms has value in itself; it has it only insofar as it involves concrete individuals. If a nation can assert itself proudly only to the detriment of its members, if a union can be created only to the detriment of those it is trying to unite, the nation or the union must be rejected. We repudiate all idealisms, mysticisms, etcetera which prefer a Form to man himself. But the matter becomes really agonizing when it is a question of a Cause which genuinely serves man. That is why the question of Stalinist politics, the problem of the relationship of the Party to the masses which it uses in order to serve them, is in the forefront of the preoccupations of all men of good will. However, there are very few who raise it without dishonesty, and we must first try to dispel a few fallacies.

The opponent of the U.S.S.R. is making use of a fallacy when, emphasizing the part of criminal violence assumed by Stalinist politics, he neglects to confront it with the ends pursued. Doubtless, the purges, the deportations, the abuses of the occupation, and the police dictatorship surpass in importance the violences practised by any other country; the very fact that there are a hundred and sixty million inhabitants in Russia multiplies the numerical coefficient of the injustices committed. But these quantitative considerations are insufficient. One can no more judge the means without the end which gives it its meaning than he can detach the end from the means which defines it. Lynching a negro or suppressing a hundred members of the opposition are two analogous acts. Lynching is an absolute evil; it represents the survival of an obsolete civilization, the perpetuation of a struggle of races which has to disappear; it is a fault without justification or excuse. Suppressing a hundred opponents is surely an outrage, but it may have meaning and a reason; it is a matter of maintaining a regime which brings to an immense mass of men a bettering of their lot. Perhaps this measure could have been avoided; perhaps it merely represents that necessary element of failure which is involved in any positive construction. It can be judged only by being replaced in the ensemble of the cause it serves.

But, on the other hand, the defender of the U.S.S.R. is making use of a fallacy when he unconditionally justifies the sacrifices and the crimes by the ends pursued; it would first be necessary to prove that, on the one hand, the end is unconditioned and that, on the other hand, the crimes committed in its name were strictly necessary. Against the death of Bukharin one counters with Stalingrad; but one would have to know to what effective

146

extent the Moscow trials increased the chances of the Russian victory. One of the ruses of Stalinist orthodoxy is, playing on the idea of necessity, to put the whole of the revolution on one side of the scale; the other side will always seem very light. But the very idea of a total dialectic of history does not imply that any factor is ever determining; on the contrary, if one admits that the life of a man may change the course of events, it is that one adheres to the conception which grants a preponderant role to Cleopatra's nose and Cromwell's wart. One is here playing, with utter dishonesty, on two opposite conceptions of the idea of necessity: one synthetic, and the other analytic; one dialectic, the other deterministic. The first makes History appear as an intelligible becoming within which the particularity of contingent accidents is reabsorbed; the dialectical sequence of the moments is possible only if there is within each moment an indetermination of the particular elements taken one by one. If, on the contrary, one grants the strict determinism of each causal series, one ends in a contingent and disordered vision of the ensemble, the conjunction of the series being brought about by chance. Therefore, a Marxist must recognize that none of his particular decisions involves the revolution in its totality; it is merely a matter of hastening or retarding its coming, of saving himself the use of other and more costly means. That does not mean that he must retreat from violence but that he must not regard it as justified *a priori* by its ends. If he considers his enterprise in its truth, that is, in its finiteness, he will understand that he has never anything but a finite stake to oppose to the sacrifices which ne calls for, and that it is an uncertain stake. Of course, this uncertainty should not keep him from pursuing his goals; but it requires that one concern himself in each case with finding a balance between the goal and its means.

Thus, we challenge every condemnation as well as every *a priori* justification of the violence practised with a view to a valid end. They must be legitimized concretely. A calm, mathematical calculation is here impossible. One must attempt to judge the chances of success that are involved in a certain sacrifice; but at the beginning this judgment will always be doubtful; besides, in the face of the immediate reality of the sacrifice, the notion of chance is difficult to think about. On the one hand, one can multiply a probability infinitely without ever reaching certainty; but yet, practically, it ends by merging with this asymptote: in our private life as in our collective life there is no other truth than a statistical one. On the other hand, the interests at stake do not allow themselves to be put into an equation; the suffering of one man, that of a million men, are incommensurable with the conquests realized by millions of others, present death is incommensurable with the life to come. It would be utopian to want to set up on the one hand the chances of success multiplied by the stake one is after, and on the other hand the weight of the immediate sacrifice. One finds himself back at the anguish of free decision. And that is why political choice is an ethical choice: it is a wager as well as a decision; one bets on the chances and risks of the measure under consideration; but whether chances and risks must be assumed or not in the given circumstances must be decided without help, and in so doing one sets up values. If in 1793 the Girondists rejected the violences of the Terror whereas a Saint-Just and a Robespierre assumed them, the reason is that they did not have the same conception of freedom. Nor was the same republic being aimed at between 1830 and 1840 by the republicans who limited themselves to a purely political opposition and those who adopted the technique of insurrection. In each case it is a matter of defining an end and realizing it, knowing that the choice of the means employed affects both the definition and the fulfillment.

Ordinarily, situations are so complex that a long analysis is necessary before being able to pose the ethical moment of the choice. We shall confine ourselves here to the consideration of a few simple examples which will enable us to make our attitude somewhat more precise. In an underground revolutionary movement when one discovers the presence of a stool-pigeon, one does not hesitate to beat him up; he is a present and future danger who has to be gotten rid of; but if a man is merely suspected of treason, the case is more ambiguous. We blame those northern peasants who in the war of 1914-18 massacred an innocent family which was suspected of signaling to the enemy; the reason is that not only were the presumptions vague, but the danger was uncertain; at any rate, it was enough to put the suspects into prison; while waiting for a serious inquiry it was easy to keep them from doing any harm. However, if a questionable individual holds the fate of other men in his hands, if, in order to avoid the risk of killing one innocent man, one runs the risk of letting ten innocent men die, it is reasonable to sacrifice him. We can merely ask that such decisions be not taken hastily and lightly, and that, all things considered, the evil that one inflicts be lesser than that which is being forestalled.

There are cases still more disturbing because there the violence is not immediately efficacious; the violences of the Resistance did not aim at the material weakening of Germany; it happens that their purpose was to create such a state of violence that collaboration would be impossible; in one sense, the burning of a whole French village was too high a price to pay for the elimination of three enemy officers; but those fires and the massacring of hostages were themselves parts of the plan; they created an abyss between the occupiers and the occupied. Likewise, the insurrections in Paris and Lyons at the beginning of the nineteenth century, or the revolts in India, did not aim at shattering the yoke of the oppressor at one blow, but rather at creating and keeping alive the meaning of the revolt and at making the mystifications of conciliation impossible. Attempts which are aware that one by one they are doomed to failure can be legitimized by the whole of the situation which they create. This is also the meaning of Steinbeck's novel *In Dubious Battle* where a communist leader does not hesitate to launch a costly strike of uncertain success but through which there will be born, along with the solidarity of the workers, the consciousness of exploitation and the will to reject it.

It seems to me interesting to contrast this example with

the debate in John Dos Passos' *The Adventures of 'a Young Man*. Following a strike, some American miners are condemned to death. Their comrades try to have their trial reconsidered. Two methods are put forward: one can act officially, and one knows that they then have an excellent chance of winning their case; one can also work up a sensational trial with the Communist Party taking the affair in hand, stirring up a press campaign and circulating international petitions; but the court will be unwilling to yield to this intimidation. The party will thereby get a tremendous amount of publicity, but the miners will be condemned. What is a man of good will to decide in this case?

Dos Passos' hero chooses to save the miners and we believe that he did right. Certainly, if it were necessary to choose between the whole revolution and the lives of two or three men, no revolutionary would hesitate; but it was merely a matter of helping along the party propaganda, or better, of increasing somewhat its chances of developing within the United States; the immediate interest of the C.P. in that country is only hypothetically tied up with that of the revolution; in fact, a cataclysm like the war has so upset the situation of the world that a great part of the gains and losses of the past have been absolutely swept away. If it is really *men* which the movement claims to be serving, in this case it must prefer saving the lives of three concrete individuals to a very uncertain and weak chance of serving a little more effectively by their sacrifice the mankind to come. If it considers these lives negligible, it is because it too ranges itself on the side of the formal politicians who prefer the Idea to its content; it is because it prefers itself, in its subjectivity, to the goals to which it claims to be dedicated. Besides, whereas in the example chosen by Steinbeck the strike is immediately an appeal to the freedom of the workers and in its very failure is already a liberation, the sacrifice of the miners is a mystification and an oppression; they are duped by being made to believe that an effort is being made to save their lives, and the whole proletariat is duped with them. Thus, in both examples, we find ourselves before the same abstract case: men are going to die so that the party which claims to be serving them will realize a limited gain; but a concrete analysis leads us to opposite moral solutions.

It is apparent that the method we are proposing, analogous in this respect to scientific or aesthetic methods, consists, in each case, of confronting the values realized with the values aimed at, and the meaning of the act with its content. The fact is that the politician, contrary to the scientist and the artist, and although the element of failure which he assumes is much more outrageous, is rarely concerned with making use of it. May it be that there is an irresistible dialectic of power wherein morality has no place? Is the ethical concern, even in its realistic and concrete form, detrimental to the interests of action? The objection will surely be made that hesitation and misgivings only impede victory. Since, in any case, there is an element of failure in all success, since the ambiguity, at any rate, must be surmounted, why not refuse to take notice of it? In the first number of the *Cahiers d'Action* a reader declared that once and for all we should regard the militant communist as "the permanent hero of our time" and should reject the exhausting tension demanded by existentialism; installed in the permanence of heroism, one will blindly direct himself toward an uncontested goal; but one then resembles Colonel de la Roque who unwaveringly went right straight ahead of him without knowing where he was going. Malaparte relates that the young Nazis, in order to become insensitive to the suffering of others, practised by plucking out the eyes of live cats; there is no more radical way of avoiding the pitfalls of ambiguity. But an action which wants to serve man ought to be careful not to forget him on the way; if it chooses to fulfill itself blindly, it will lose its meaning or will take on an unforeseen meaning; for the goal is not fixed once and for all; it is defined all along the road which leads to it. Vigilance alone can keep alive the validity of the goals and the genuine assertion of freedom. Moreover, ambiguity can not fail to appear on the scene; it is felt by the victim, and his revolt or his complaints also make it exist for his tyrant; the latter will then be tempted to put everything into question, to renounce, thus denying both himself and his ends; or, if he persists, he will continue to blind himself only by multiplying crimes and by perverting his original design more and more. The fact is that the man of action becomes a dictator not in respect to his ends but because these ends are necessarily set up through his will. Hegel, in his *Phenomenology,* has emphasized this inextricable confusion between objectivity and subjectivity. A man gives himself to a Cause only by making it *his*

Cause; as he fulfills himself within it, it is also through him that it is expressed, and the will to power is not distinguished in such a case from generosity; when an individual or a party chooses to triumph, whatever the cost may be, it is their own triumph which they take for an end. If the fusion of the Commissar and the Yogi were realized, there would be a self-criticism in the man of action which would expose to him the ambiguity of his will, thus arresting the imperious drive of his subjectivity and, by the same token, contesting the unconditioned value of the goal. But the fact is that the politician follows the line of least resistance; it is easy to fall asleep over the unhappiness of others and to count it for very little; it is easier to throw a hundred men, ninety-seven of whom are innocent, into prison, than to discover the three culprits who are hidden among them; it is easier to kill a man than to keep a close watch on him; all politics makes use of the police, which officially flaunts its radical contempt for the individual and which loves violence for its own sake. The thing that goes by the name of political necessity is in part the laziness and brutality of the police. That is why it is incumbent upon ethics not to follow the line of least resistance; an act which is not destined, but rather quite freely consented to; it must make itself effective so that what was at first facility may become difficult. For want of internal criticism, this is the role that an opposition must take upon itself. There are two types of opposition. The first is a rejection of the very ends set up by a regime: it is the opposition of anti-fascism to fascism, of fascism to socialism. In the second type, the oppositionist

154

accepts the objective goal but criticizes the subjective movement which aims at it; he may not even wish for a change of power, but he deems it necessary to bring into play a contestation which will make the subjective appear as such. Thereby he exacts a perpetual contestation of the means by the end and of the end by the means. He must be careful himself not to ruin, by the means which he employs, the end he is aiming at, and above all not to pass into the service of the oppositionists of the first type. But, delicate as it may be, his role is, neverthless, necessary. Indeed, on the one hand, it would be absurd to oppose a liberating action with the pretext that it implies crime and tyranny; for without crime and tyranny there could be no liberation of man; one can not escape that dialectic which goes from freedom to freedom through dictatorship and oppression. But, on the other hand, he would be guilty of allowing the liberating movement to harden into a moment which is acceptable only if it passes into its opposite; tyranny and crime must be kept from triumphantly establishing themselves in the world; the conquest of freedom is their only justification, and the assertion of freedom against them must therefore be kept alive.

Conclusion

[handwritten note: This kind of ethics is individualist but not solipsistic. Individual defined in his relationship to the world & others]

Is this kind of ethics individualistic or not? Yes, if one means by that that it accords to the individual an absolute value and that it recognizes in him alone the power of laying the foundations of his own existence. It is individualism in the sense in which the wisdom of the ancients, the Christian ethics of salvation, and the Kantian ideal of virtue also merit this name; it is opposed to the totalitarian doctrines which raise up beyond man the mirage of Mankind. But it is not solipsistic, since the individual is defined only by his relationship to the world and to other individuals; he exists only by transcending himself, and his freedom can be achieved only through the freedom of others. He justifies his existence by a movement which, like freedom, springs from his heart but which leads outside of him.

This individualism does not lead to the anarchy of personal whim. Man is free; but he finds his law in his very freedom. First, he must assume his freedom and not flee it; he assumes it by a constructive movement: one does not exist without doing something; and also by a negative movement which rejects oppression for oneself and others. In construction, as in rejection, it is a matter of reconquering freedom on the contingent facticity of existence, that is, of taking the given, which, at the start, *is there* without any reason, as something willed by man.

[handwritten notes in margins: Man finds his law in freedom / must assume]

156

[handwritten notes at bottom:
1) constructive moment — acts
2) negative moment — rejects oppression for oneself & others
Both moments is a reconquering of contingent facticity — given but willed by man]

A conquest of this kind is never finished; the contingency remains, and, so that he may assert his will, man is even obliged to stir up in the world the outrage he does not want. But this element of failure is a very condition of his life; one can never dream of eliminating it without immediately dreaming of death. This does not mean that one should consent to failure, but rather one must consent to struggle against it without respite.

its failure is condition of his life

Yet, isn't this battle without victory pure gullibility? It will be argued that this is only a ruse of transcendance projecting before itself a goal which constantly recedes, running after itself on an endless treadmill; to exist for Mankind is to remain where one is, and it fools itself by calling this turbulent stagnation progress; our whole ethics does nothing but encourage it in this lying enterprise since we are asking each one to confirm existence as a value for all others; isn't it simply a matter of organizing among men a complicity which allows them to substitute a game of illusions for the given world?

We have already attempted to answer this objection. One can formulate it only by placing himself on the grounds of an inhuman and consequently false objectivity; within Mankind men may be fooled; the word "lie" has a meaning by opposition to the truth established by men themselves, but Mankind can not fool itself completely since it is precisely Mankind which creates the criteria of true and false. In Plato, art is mystification because there is the heaven of Ideas; but in the earthly domain all glorification of the earth is true as soon as it is realized. Let men attach value to words, forms, colors,

mathematical theorems, physical laws, and athletic pro-
wess; let them accord value to one another in love and
friendship, and the objects, the events, and the men immediately *have* this value; they have it absolutely. It is
possible that a man may refuse to love anything on earth;
he will prove this refusal and he will carry it out by suicide. If he lives, the reason is that, whatever he may say,
there still remains in him some attachment to existence;
his life will be commensurate with this attachment; it
will justify itself to the extent that it genuinely justifies
the world.

This justification, though open upon the entire universe
through time and space, will always be finite. Whatever
one may do, one never realizes anything but a limited
work, like existence itself which tries to establish itself
through that work and which death also limits. It is the
assertion of our finiteness which doubtless gives the
doctrine which we have just evoked its austerity and, in
some eyes, its sadness. As soon as one considers a system
abstractly and theoretically, one puts himself, in effect,
on the plane of the universal, thus, of the infinite. That is
why reading the Hegelian system is so comforting. I
remember having experienced a great feeling of calm on
reading Hegel in the impersonal framework of the Bi-
bliotheque Nationale in August 1940. But once I got into
the street again, into my life, out of the system, beneath
a real sky, the system was no longer of any use to me: what
it had offered me, under a show of the infinite, was the
consolations of death; and I again wanted to live in the
midst of living men. I think that, inversely, existentialism

does not offer to the reader the consolations of an abstract evasion: existentialism proposes no evasion. On the contrary, its ethics is experienced in the truth of life, and it then appears as the only proposition of salvation which one can address to men. Taking on its own account Descartes' revolt against the evil genius, the pride of the thinking reed in the face of the universe which crushes him, it asserts that, despite his limits, through them, it is up to each one to fulfill his existence as an absolute. Regardless of the staggering dimensions of the world about us, the density of our ignorance, the risks of catastrophes to come, and our individual weakness within the immense collectivity, the fact remains that we are absolutely free today if we choose to will our existence in its finiteness, a finiteness which is open on the infinite. And in fact, any man who has known real loves, real revolts, real desires, and real will knows quite well that he has no need of any outside guarantee to be sure of his goals; their certitude comes from his own drive. There is a very old saying which goes: "Do what you must, come what may." That amounts to saying in a different way that the result is not external to the good will which fulfills itself in aiming at it. If it came to be that each man did what he must, existence would be saved in each one without there being any need of dreaming of a paradise where all would be reconciled in death.

Index